Sacred Portals:
Pathways to the Self

By

Constance S. Rodriguez, PhD

This book is a work of non-fiction. Names and places have been changed to protect the privacy of all individuals. The events and situations are true.

ISBN: 1-4033-7591-7 (e-book)
ISBN: 1-4033-7592-5 (Paperback)

Library of Congress Control Number: 2002094582

This book is printed on acid free paper.

Printed in the United States of America
Bloomington, IN

Cover Photo courtesy of MJ Photography

Excerpts from *Spiritual Healing: Doctors Examine Therapeutic Touch and Other Holistic Treatments,* by Dora Kunz, Copyright 1995 Quest books/The Theosophical Publishing House, Ill. Reprinted by permission.

Excerpts from *Radical Nature: Rediscovering the Soul of Matter*, by Christian de Quincey, Reprinted by permission.

1stBooks - rev. 09/17/03

Acknowledgments

Birthing a book has been a lot like traveling through a labyrinth. There are twists and turns and dead ends. One path would feel like it would lead me to the center, but instead, I would have to begin again. Moving into the material and out again has been a deepening experience for me, and many have been with me along the way. My sincere appreciation goes to these people who have helped me, especially to my husband, whose unwavering support and encouragement always came just at the right time. I am particularly grateful for his photographic skills as his keen eye gifted me with the cover photo of this book. I want to thank my son, Bryan Rodriguez, for his computer wizardry and for his patience and fortitude, and my appreciation goes to my daughter, Alicia Rodriguez, for her insightful skills and word wizardry.

I also want to give special recognition and gratitude to my many friends who lent their love and support, most especially Virginia Rose, who was always available to hear me when I needed to be heard. My deep gratitude goes to Anya Lawrence, Yashi Johnson, Georgia Dow, Joan Goddard and Marty Cottler, Jeff Cram, friends and colleagues who provided a critical eye and valuable feedback during various phases of the gestation period—often when I most needed it. Thank you sincerely. Special appreciation is also due to Penny Peirce who has given me valuable feedback and support for this project. A special thank you goes to Dianne Skafte, whose oracular mentoring provided silent encouragement to venture forth into these unknown realms. Last but not least, is a grateful appreciation to my editor, Pat Hadley-Miller, whose eagle eye finely tuned every bend in the manuscript labyrinth.

I also wish to thank my wonderful dream and sandplay groups whose years of participation with me seeded the underpinnings for this book, as well as all those who anonymously participated in the creation of this book by gifting me with your stories and life experience, for without you, this birthing wouldn't have taken place.

Table of Contents

Exercises

Prologue

It was Valentine's Day and I had just returned home from an evening out with my sweetheart, my husband of 33 years. The phone rang and I answered,

"Hello, is this Connie?'

"Yes it is."

"This is Susan Anderson. You sent me your proposal and I wanted to talk to you about it."

My mind went into confusion. I had sent out several query letters, but only the day before—in the afternoon—had I sent one proposal out. My mind was working to put it together. How could she have gotten my proposal in such a short time—and read it?

"I am interested in your ideas, but I have to tell you it's a bit esoteric. People want the 'how to's," Susan said. "If you can put together a 'how to book' on developing intuition, I would be interested in talking with you further. After all, you want it to get published, right?"

Susan was the first agent I had ever talked with, and I was grateful for her insight, but a "how to" on accessing threshold states of consciousness? After I hung up the phone, I told my husband what she had suggested, and said, "I don't know how to tell people how to."

"Yes, you do," he said simply.

I went to bed with this on my mind. Susan's suggestion seemed impossible. This book is about the soul, and finding yourself through threshold experiences while in non-ordinary states of consciousness.

How do you teach someone how to do that? I woke up in the middle of the night flooded with "how to's."

Throughout this book you will find the keys of psychonoetic tools for accessing these states and the last chapter is devoted to specific exercises and steps to waking your inner knowing. Psychonoetic means "soul knowing." Psyche is a Greek word meaning "soul," and noetic means "to know." This book is not a book on how to become psychic, but rather how to become and stay connected to an inner awareness that will guide you through your life. Opening these doors is transformational, and though I give you steps toward this endeavor, know that they may not always be easy.

This book is for you if you want to learn the "how-to's" to awakening the psychonoetic self: the perceptual nature that resides in everyone. This book is also for you if you are curious about the nature of subtle energy fields and how they are related to your health and your intuitive self. But more to the point, it is about the soul's journey and finding your way on the path to your inner knowing.

I would like to tell you about a few of the assumptions I hold regarding this material. One of the assumptions I make is that we are a soul with a body. We have come to the Earth plane for our evolution and for the experience we can only gain while here. I also make the assumption that the psyche exists outside of the body and merely inhabits the body for a relatively short time. The body is, however, not a useless object to be worn like a space suit. It is actually the antennae for our learning and evolution and therefore is sacred and to be honored for the wonderful way it helps us to "learn." The body has several bodies, or energy bodies, that make up the subtle body, and this subtle body is the reason we are able to enter and experience multiple dimensions: the threshold realms.

I also make the assumption that every thing is animate and has "chi," or energy, as well as a level of consciousness. This is a fairly new stance not held within Newtonian thought and science, but is part of the new paradigm sweeping the United States and hopefully the planet. And finally, "spiritual" does not mean that it has anything to do with religion as we know it. Carolyn Myss, author and medical intuitive, states that religion is formed to protect the "tribe" and spirituality is an individual experience. Itzhak Bentov, author of *Stalking the Wild Pendulum*, states it has to do with "the development and refinement of the nervous system and the accompanying rise in the level of consciousness, which has reached a point in frequency high enough on the scale of the quality of consciousness to resonate with the highest levels of creation. This automatically entails the development of inner moral values and the development of the heart."[1]

Hank Wesselman, author of *Visionseeker*, states that these beliefs and values constitute the core of a new worldview that is being shared by an ever-increasing number of people in the West. He quotes a study that resulted in 24 percent of the population answering a survey. In the spring of 1996, the preliminary results of a national American Lives Survey, conducted by sociologist Paul Ray and sponsored by the Institute of Noetic Sciences and the Fetzer Institute, revealed that in the U.S. alone, 44 million Americans fall into this category of holding a new worldview. According to Ray, this group represents a "larger population of socially concerned, environmentally aware, and spiritually focused creative people, who are carriers of more positive ideas, values, and trends than any pervious renaissance period in history."[2]

Another consideration I made while writing this book is the choice of words regarding "higher." It seems that in our culture the word higher has become synonymous with "better." I have struggled with other words to better describe these notions, but have on occasion continued to use them because they do imply the sense of what I mean. In referring to the "Higher Self" I have usually left this in or have referred to a larger source or an ultimate Self. Throughout this book you will see that I use the lowercase self to signify the ego self, our everyday self. The capitalized Self refers to a transpersonal Self, Oversoul or "Higher Self." When referring to a higher vibration, I am referring to a finer vibration, which resonates at a faster speed. This is not always the state in which we want to find ourselves, for example moving into an altered state means reducing our brain waves to a slower pace!

Carl C. Jung, a Swiss psychiatrist and visionary, was a man ahead of his time. Many of his ideas and theories are embedded in my thinking and understanding of the material in this book becoming the foundation for much that follows. His revolutionary ideas, alongside of Freud's, have shaped our thinking with regard to psychology.

However I have found that psychology falls short when we examine the multidimensional universe. Because Jungian terminology is often found mostly in Jungian material, I have included a glossary for those of you unfamiliar with these sometimes-obscure terms.

Also, all names and outer life descriptions mentioned in this book have been changed to preserve the anonymity of those who have shared their stories. However, all of the stories are true to the experience and I have done my best to relay them as they have happened. You may find that many of these stories have an echo of truth for you as well, or you may find that you have your own stories to tell, which I would love to hear. See the back of the book for ways to contact me.

Introduction

Journey into the Threshold Realms

Any moment can be a turning point, but some periods are momentous and bring all aspects of life and specters of death to the crossroads of awareness.
-Michael Mead *(Author and Poet)*

I wasn't born "psychic." Nor did I have an accident, coma or bump on the head that opened my perceptual sense-abilities. I was just an average person wanting to know how to develop these faculties, probably just like you.

There was a time when I couldn't "see" anything. I remember going to a dream class where the teacher led us all in a meditation. She asked us to allow an image to form of something we wanted from the class. Try as I might, I couldn't get an image. To my great consternation, nothing came to me. I wanted to imagine one, yet still I was in the dark, literally. As we went around sharing our images, everyone else seemed to get something, and some of the images were grand. One woman saw a golden bowl with a white dove flying out of it. When it was my turn to share, I had nothing to say.

During this period of my life, I decided I would take a psychic class. In this class we were to find our own way of getting information. The teacher took us through our sensate functions to feel energy, our visual functions to see, and how to use our clairaudient function to hear. In the second class, I centered myself in meditation and quickly slipped into a deep altered state. Suddenly, I felt a huge rush of energy fill my body, and I felt far away. The person I was in dyad with had asked a question. Out of my mouth came a loud, authoritative voice. It felt very masculine. I heard it giving her a lecture about her life and wasting time. Afterward, I was shaken and embarrassed. Silence permeated the small room and everyone's eyes were on me. Finally, the teacher said, "We don't teach channeling at this school." I wanted to run out of the room that minute. To her credit the teacher did talk about channeling and said it was a gift that couldn't be taught.

I was overwhelmed by the extraordinary energy that had suddenly come into my body. And furthermore, I didn't like the feeling of something or someone else coming in and taking over. I only wanted to be able to "see," and channeling wasn't a part of my plan in any way. Plus, having my cynic fully on board, I was very mistrustful of channeling at that time.

So that ended my psychic career so to speak. I was fearful for years after that experience of going "into trance." It has taken me more years and lots of work to undo the somatic, albeit irrational, fear of being drowned, hung on the nearest tree, or worse—being burnt at the nearest stake (fears that leak through from the collective unconscious or past lives that are stored in cellular and/or unconscious memory). Not to mention that my family-of-origin's alcoholic constellation made being in control a prime motivation in my life. Thankfully all of this took me on a journey, which I want to share with you, stopping along the way to give you practical keys to developing your own inner awareness through these tools.

Early in my work as a psychotherapist, I noticed the ability to follow the images of others when leading them into their own imagery. I also began to notice that it seemed as if images would pop into my head, and as I shared them, my clients responded that they were the exact image needed for the situation. As this "ability" began to unfold, I noticed that I was able to watch the imagery as I led my clients into guided visualizations. Upon their return I would ask about the imagery and often it would be similar if not exactly like the client's experiences.

One of these times a woman was telling me of her early childhood molestation by her father. I asked her if she could go back to that scene and—in the privacy of her mind— rework it. I quietly waited until she had completed with the imagery. As she sat with her eyes closed, I could "see" a young girl pushing a man into the trunk of an old model, green-colored car and shove it into a river. When she opened her tear-filled eyes, I asked her to tell me what happened.

She said, "this time, when my father was taking me to the woods to rape me, I was able to grab him and shoved him into the trunk!"

"Then what happened?" I asked.

"I pushed the car into the river."

"What kind of car was it?"

"It was a 1947 green Studebaker." I was astonished! It was one of the first times I knew I had watched the imagery unfold like a movie reel in the imaginal realm. How does this happen? This became a guiding question that has led me to explore the threshold realms in non-ordinary states of consciousness.

I have always felt blessed to be able to watch the scenes as they unfold in these threshold states. The sense of being there is very real for me as well, and often it is like I am standing over one's shoulder, or nearby, watching all that is taking place. I seem to have a "wider" vision of the surround than what the person is experiencing. When I ask about the surround, for example, it is as if the "screen" opens to them as well.

Sacred Portals is about opening doors into the psyche to awaken your inner knowing, which will lead you to your authentic self. It is also about learning how to fine-tune your state of consciousness in order to accommodate the vibrational nature in the universal energy fields, which is one of the keys to knowing your inner self. Accessing the interactive fields in the vibrational universe is important because of the transformative energy and its numinosity that occurs while in these betwixt and between places. The root word of numinosity is *numen*, a Latin word meaning a god. Numinosity conveys an illumination; it is a felt, live experience that transforms the experiencer. When in its presence, everyone feels it. It is like an electrical charge and you know you have been touched by something beyond your everyday world. Your world will be forever illuminated vis-à-vis that experience.

Sacred Portals is also about the interface between Earth's energy and our bodies as tuning devices, which are *gateways* that lead you to synchronistic experiences. In this book you will learn how to activate these gateways and how to bring them into your life in specific ways. Threshold experiences are unforgettable, numinous experiences that will open you more fully to who you are.

I believe that each threshold state is a bandwidth of energy with its own vibratory signature. We can access these states by learning how to recognize each octave through our own tuning device—the body. You will not only learn about the multiple gateways available to you, but also, you will receive guidance and exercises to do throughout the book to develop your perceptual senses as a part of the journey to Self.

Not only do I share with you my personal story of discovering the healing power of threshold states, but I also tell many stories of others' experiences to give you solid ground in the landscape of threshold realms. I also have included several exercises throughout the chapters for you to use if you wish while reading this book. Threshold places feel sacred as one encounters the numinous, live energy encountered in these experiences occurring in many forms, each a zone, or dimension unto itself. They occur in the outer world and the inner world of the psyche and at some points, it is impossible to make a distinction between the two! This book gives you an understanding of thresholds and how to invite experiences of them into your life. Although I realize that each chapter could be a book in itself, I feel that each is important to the journey toward inner knowing.

Chapter One looks at thresholds as portals into imaginal realms and orients you to the universal mind. This chapter sets a theoretical stage for the rest of the book; following with stories that make it come alive. It also gives examples of synchronicity, and ways of inviting it more fully into your life. It shows you how the psyche is not restricted by time constructs that we normally impose upon it in this time-bound, consensual reality. In this chapter we see how the psyche moves about freely in the thresholds of other-world realms, and how synchronicity then becomes a part of the journey once you have opened up to the energetic vibration that lives outside the linear way of being in the world.

The second chapter moves deeper into many dimensions of the psyche, which is home to the collective unconscious. You will see how the imaginal region of the psyche is one of the various dimensions through which you may travel as a pathway to the Self. It offers examples of how oracular consciousness works, it informs you of the importance of Carl G. Jung's discovery of the collective unconscious, and the archetypal fields as threshold experiences. In this rich inner world you will be introduced to the archetypal field as paramount to understanding threshold states and how they actively influence us both in waking reality and dream life. I also provide you with some history of dreams and the role they have played as doorways into the collective unconscious and archetypal realms.

✓ Chapter Three is situated in the scientific world. The chapter focuses on the mechanics of how it is we can live in a multidimensional universe. It supports the premise that energy fields found in nature are energetic vibrations that can be felt, seen by intuitives, accessed, and even altered. And further, when we come in contact with particular kinds of fields—subtle fields—we are often moved or changed by the experience. For those of you who are more satisfied with the linear world of quantum physics (an oxymoron), you may enjoy the development of these ideas and notions about the way the world works at the quantum levels. If you prefer more of a meandering path, you can skip this chapter and still enjoy the journey.

With the foundation laid in quantum physics in the previous chapter, Chapter Four invites you to enter the world of holographic journeying. It is about people who have entered this kind of threshold experience and who have been truly transformed from the experience. It is a virtual reality that brings you into a new relationship with yourself. You will see how people's lives have been changed from this work. From dramatic transformations that unleash the blocked patterns people have struggled with most of their lives to awakenings about the changes they feel ready to make after this kind of work. Usually known as "past-life" work, I take you past the linear paradigm, and propose that we are entering a realm of virtual possibilities by allowing the psyche to time travel to where it needs to go for balance and healing.

In Chapter Five you will learn what it means to find your own inner guidance in these threshold states. In Chapter Two, I introduce you to dreams as portals into the imaginal realm. In this chapter I will give you keys to unlock the mystery of your dream world to find meaning and inner guidance through them. Throughout the centuries, these oft-traveled realms are well known by shamen in many cultures. We will explore the world of the shaman, master of threshold states. Through examples and stories you will not only learn how others have found their inner guides but also methods of travel to the inner worlds.

Chapter Six focuses on waking the perceptual self through the subtle body energy fields of the physical body. In this chapter I explain how the body is a harmonic receiver ready to receive information from the universe if it is properly tuned. I give you detailed descriptions of how these bodies of light influence you. The light body is an essential key to your intuition and health. You will learn how it interfaces with universal energy fields to engage threshold states.

Chapter Seven focuses in-depth on *how* to access these many portals. A few specific keys will help you to unlock these doors. I also give you steps that will lead you to your own inner worlds where extraordinary experiences can transform your life. In this chapter, you will learn psychonoetic tools and exercises for clearing your field and chakras, and why this is important, not only for developing keen inner knowing, but also how this is important for the evolution of your consciousness as well. I will give you caveats to be aware of as well as tools to learn the difference between imagination and true inner guidance.

The last chapter is a synthesis of your journey through the inner and outer thresholds and interdimensional realms you have visited while reading this book. We will integrate the tapestry leading to your central core. My hope is that you will have new tools to take you further into your soul's path. My wish is that you will also live with the magic that becomes a daily part of life when invoking your perceptual awareness. Bon voyage!

Chapter One

Across the Borders of Time

The Western mind must be willing to open itself to a reality the nature of which could shatter its most established beliefs about itself and the world. This is where the real act of heroism is going to be. A threshold must now be crossed, a threshold demanding a courageous act of faith, of imagination of trust in a larger and more complex reality; a threshold, moreover, demanding an act of unflinching self-discernment.

> -Rick Tarnas *The Passion of the Western Mind*

There are places in this world that are neither here nor there, neither up nor down, neither real nor imaginary. These are the in-between places, difficult to find and even more challenging to sustain. Yet, they are the most fruitful places of all.

> -Thomas Moore *Care of the Soul*

21

Thresholds

I was sitting with Debbie in my office as she expressed her all-too-familiar grief at the loss of a relationship, one she was hoping would meet her heart's longing. As her therapist, empathetically I sat next to her as she placed her grief—in the form of symbolic miniatures—into the sandtray, which is a small sand box that holds images created by the miniatures in psychotherapeutic work.

The last symbol she chose from my shelf was a small wolf, with its head up in the recognizable stance of a howl. Just as she placed the miniature wolf into the center of the tray, a dog in the neighborhood began to howl. We sat there and looked at each other in stunned disbelief while its haunting howl lasted for nearly five minutes. Tears came to her eyes, and I sat with chills moving up and down my body. In its synchronistic way, nature echoed her grief as we sat and listened in that numinous moment. Never before in the ten years of practice in this office, nor since, have I heard a dog howl.

Transpersonal moments seem to cross the borders of time, reaching out and touching us in profound ways. What is it that moves us, awakens us, or shifts our awareness, maybe only for that moment, maybe even permanently, forever leaving us with a knowing about another place or realm that lives outside the everyday mind's eye?

I refer to these moments that reach into another dimension as threshold experiences: experiences that change our mind, and transform our notion of who we are.

I have always had a fascination with doors and doorways. They represent portals that can open the way to richness and meaning in one's life. Thresholds hold a mystery; a mystery that lives in a neither/nor place. Thresholds are not only sacred and mysterious places, but are also places of great fear, incubation and gestation. When we move into a threshold place, we leave *Chronos*, or linear time, and enter *Kairos*, or timelessness. We enter into liminal time. Liminal comes from the Latin root word *limen*, which means threshold.

Threshold places are rites of passages that are often sought through ritual, plant medicines, and ceremony. Places of power can be found at sacred sites on the planet and serve as portals moving us from the profane into the profound. Places where the veil between worlds is thin become places where the unknown becomes known.

A threshold is an in-between place, a place between worlds. It is neither here nor there. It is not the outside world, nor the inside. We are most familiar with crossing a threshold everyday when we enter or exit our home or other buildings. Many cultures are superstitious when it comes to entering doorways. They are seen as cracks between worlds where simple to elaborate rituals have been created to stave off the creatures from Otherworlds that threaten to enter when the threshold is crossed.

In Ireland great care was taken before entering the home. Author, Mara Freeman, in an article on thresholds, states, "The Earthen floor just inside the threshold of old Irish cottages in the south and west was known as the 'welcome of the door.' Upon entering, a visitor would stand here and say a blessing for the household. This was holy ground, and dirt scraped from it was good for curing a number of ills. An in-between place, it was sacred because it marked the boundary between the life of the human family within and the wide world without. It was neither here nor there, and so it allowed a crack to open between the worlds where power could seep in."[1] In Ireland today, you can see the honoring of the threshold by the cheerful doors painted in bright colors.

In Europe, gargoyles can still be seen mounted on the top of old buildings and churches in Europe. Traditionally, these monstrous-looking animals guarded the inside, keeping evil spirits at bay. In Celtic traditions, homes were protected by various symbols and means. Freeman states that symbols on the doorposts—sprigs of rowan wood, St. Brighid's crosses, horseshoes hung up on the lintel—all served to insulate the house against too much voltage.[2] Traveling through Great Britain today, you can still see horseshoes and other ornaments adorning the lintel of the door.

In our culture, the bridegroom traditionally carries the bride over the threshold of the door just after the wedding. This marks the beginning of a new life, a transition from virgin to wife, from single to wed, and symbolizes the sacred union and vows the couple made to honor their new life together. It also served to protect the wife from evil spirits. Threshold places are thought to be dangerous because they are seen as where the veil between worlds is thin. This crossing must be done with intention and care. Malidoma Somé of the Dogan tribe in Africa says that we must be protected and ready to enter the Otherworld realms.

Once, while in Tobago, a third world country, I attended a church gathering and worship. The people from the village infused traditional ancient tribal rituals with Christian worship. The day of worship began with prayers and after a few hours, heated up with members speaking in tongues, dancing and writhing in the middle of the floor. It was quite stimulating and wonderful. On the day I attended, I came early enough to see that on every doorway a cross—which looked like an "x"—was chalk-marked on the ground. I noticed that each member of the village who came through a doorway bent over and touched the marking, then made the sign of the cross on their body. I later realized that they were honoring the sacred space as they entered the church's interior space. I asked about the "x" on the ground and was told it was to keep "evil spirits from entering."

Mircea Eliade, a renowned author and expert in rites of passage, symbols and initiation, states that "the threshold is the limit, the boundary, the frontier that distinguishes and opposes two worlds—and at the same time the paradoxical place where those worlds communicate, where passage from the profane to the sacred world becomes possible." [3]

Anatomy of the Psyche

Hawaiian medicine people teach that there are four levels of reality. Author Hank Wesselman says that they know of even more, but that these four are the levels we need to currently concern ourselves with. Shamanic traditions teach of three worlds: the upper world, lower world, and middle world. Rudolf Steiner has written extensively about the nature of "higher" dimensions and planes of existence. Steiner states that there are seven "regions" in the higher dimensions. Tenth century mystic, Ibn'Arabi speaks of five planes in the *mundus imaginalis*, or world of the imaginal. In Chapter Two I will give you an in-depth look at the imaginal realm. These regions or realms have vibrational signatures that can be accessed through meditative states, or in non-ordinary states of consciousness.

These are threshold places that are intermediate realms that have subtle differences in how they "feel" at each level. The psyche, having both conscious and unconscious states, is often thought of as being on a continuum between these two poles. However, this is too simplistic. When we are in a very focused state of attention our psyche's antennae can be picking up other information outside of our immediate awareness. And conversely, when we are in a diffused state of consciousness our psyche can be picking up very succinct information. Therefore, when speaking of the multidimensionality of the psyche, I am speaking to all of these aspects of the personal psyche as well as the world psyche—or collective psyche—and all of its relative dimensions. I am referring to "fields" of consciousness.

William James, a philosopher of religion wrote about the field and its surround in the early 1900s. He said, "it lies around us like a *magnetic field*, inside of which our centre of energy turns like a compass-needle, as the present phase of consciousness alters into its successor. Our whole past store of memories floats beyond this margin, ready at a touch to come in; and the entire mass of residual powers, impulses, and knowledges [sic] that constitute our empirical self stretches continuously beyond it." (*Emphasis added*)[4]

I like the image of a magnetic field "ready at a touch to come in." Have you ever had the experience of chills or goose bumps for no apparent reason? That is my experience of how the field makes itself known. It is like vibrational keys that when "touched" become activating sources that allow us entrance into the realms of the unknown, sometimes frightening, sometimes ecstatic, always awe-full.

Synchronicity: A Hole in the Fabric of Time

Just when you need a taxi in the middle of nowhere, one shows up. A person you have not seen in ages, but were just thinking of, calls out of the blue. A woman dreams of an unusual cat, who in waking time has no affinity to cats. The following day she is in a small antique shop where a cat comes in, rubs up against her legs and won't leave her side while she is in the shop. These kinds of moments are referred to as synchronistic events.

The example of the numinous moment that opened this chapter is also an example of synchronicity. Synchronicity is often described as when two seemingly unrelated events occur at the same moment in time. A numinous experience is any experience that has a sacred and private sense for the person. It stirs the soul, is difficult to express, and is often a transformative moment or experience. Sometimes you can have a numinous experience that is not synchronistic—for example, a dream can be numinous—and vice versa. A synchronistic event may or may not have the sacred and profoundly unspeakable sense, like the howling wolf/dog.

When we are touched by the sacred through a numinous event we are forever changed. Psychoanalyst Lionel Corbett in his book *The Religious Function of the Psyche* states that the numinosum "is an attempt to initiate the person into a higher state of consciousness" and that it always produces a state of humility.[5] The manifestation of the numinous comes from a larger order; one that feels like it comes from outside ourselves. It has an archetypal feeling, as if it is produced by the gods, by a divine order. Once we have been touched by the numinous, we long for its return. It becomes, as Corbett emphasizes, a religious experience.

I love the idea that synchronicity can be thought of as the place where psyche meets matter at an intersection in the fabric of time, where a "hole" in space-time opens and transforms us as well as our world. Often synchronistic events seem numinous; however, as pointed out earlier, not all of them are. Synchronistic events seem to occur when the ego, or sense of self, has been slightly dismantled or worse.

Several years ago I went to Tobago, a small island in the southern most tip of the Caribbean, where many synchronistic events occurred. On one of the days that I was there, I actually had the experience of a taxi appearing out of nowhere. I had walked several miles to a village to be able attend a day of ritual. As the day wore on, I began to feel unwell, and thought I should head back to my lodging. Walking along a narrow road in the stifling humid climate, I thought I would have to rest every few hundreds yards until I got back. As I was pondering my situation, I wished fervently for a taxi, but knew that it was only wishful thinking, because all taxis stayed on the one outer road that outlined the tiny island. Just then I looked up and to my amazement, there was an outer island taxi slowly making its way toward me. It stopped right beside me and rolling down the window, the driver asked in his Tobagan lilt, "Would ya be needin' a taxi?" I couldn't believe my good luck. After hopping in and letting him know where I was staying, I asked him why he happened to be coming down that road. He told me he was on his way home for lunch, just like he did every day. What kind of divine intervention made it possible for that to happen just at that moment, on that particular road? There were many little roads and streets I could have taken back. Although this encounter was very synchronistic—and wonderful—it was not all that numinous.

Carl G. Jung, the Swiss psychiatrist, and father of Jungian psychology, described synchronistic events as "an acausal connecting principle that manifests itself through meaningful coincidences." He thought that people as well as all animate and inanimate objects were linked through a collective unconscious. Just as modern atomic physics acknowledges that the researcher affects whatever he or she studies at the particle level, Jung suggested that the psyche of the observing person interacts in the moment with the events of the outside world.

Indigenous cultures have known this all along. They have not lost the innate connection with Earth as a sentient being, or *animus mundi,* world soul. Malidoma Somé, whom I referred to earlier, is an African leader in the men's movement and speaker in the United States on ritual and rites of passage. He states that the white man has lost touch with his ancestors and is therefore lost to himself. We have become robotic slaves and time and technology have become our masters. Many of us have forgotten what it is like to live within the moment, in that effortless state of being where the mystery and numinosity of life exist and where synchronicity lives.

Synchronicity occurred often on Tobago, and I became fascinated by these events because they seemed so commonplace. When I first arrived, there were so many new and unexpected experiences common to third world travel that I struggled, feeling very vulnerable. However, after a few days, I sunk totally into this ego-less state of being and enjoyed what felt like a state of grace. That is when I noticed that synchronicities manifested every time I was in this state of grace, an effortless state that seems to be the norm in Tobago, which felt as if a greater knowingness was orchestrating the events. Once I surrendered my task-oriented controlling ego to this greater knowing and relaxed into trusting, anything that was needed seemed to magically appear. It was actually quite wonderful. Later, upon reflection, I noticed that I had felt out of sorts and off "center." This off-centeredness was really due to being forced into a state of not-knowing. I wonder now if this also is a part of the sense of grace, and a key to the manifestation of synchronicity.

Another major experience of a synchronistic—and numinous—event occurred the first day of our journey to Tobago. Our group flew into San Juan, Puerto Rico, to catch a connecting flight to Tobago; however, our flight was late and we missed our connection. This meant that we had a 24-hour layover in San Juan, which provided us the opportunity to explore the island.

My 25-year-old daughter, Alicia, had decided at the last minute to join us in Tobago; however, she was unable to travel on the same airline, and in fact, was coming a day later. Because of our delay, unbeknownst to her, it turned out that I would be able to meet her at the airport in San Juan and continue to Tobago together. That morning our group went to Old Town in San Juan, while I headed back to the airport to meet Alicia. Because of security, the arrival gates in the San Juan airport are glassed in and I had to wait for her in another area of the airport. As I waited, I did not see her come out of the area for deplaning passengers. When she did not get off the plane, I became frantic; to make matters worse, the airline checked the passenger list and told me that she had never boarded the plane. At this point, I was beyond frantic and called my husband to see if he could contact her airline agent to possibly track what could have happened. He told me to call him back in exactly an hour and fifteen minutes.

In the meantime, I had to decide whether to just wait there at the airport, to go back to my hotel, or to head up to Old Town to wait out the hour. Needless to say, I was extremely distraught and not in the mood to enjoy the sights. However, I decided I would go to Old Town in hopes of finding some of my group members, who had told me that they were going to start out in an area of Old Town called *Parque de la Palomas,* or "Park of the Birds." I hailed a cab and told him of my destination. Once in Old Town I was amazed at how large it was. There were literally streets upon streets of shops in every direction. It could have been five miles wide and long, and reminded me somewhat of Market Square in San Francisco. I was overwhelmed at the thought of trying to find anyone from my group and thought I would just hang around a phone booth once I found one. The other problem was that it was extremely busy, and we were just inching along in traffic. I was feeling anxious and told the cabby to just let me out and I would walk. He pointed me in the general direction of the park. Wouldn't you know it, but as soon as I stepped out of the cab, it began to rain, then pour! I was dressed only in shorts and sandals, not even having a jacket or umbrella. I felt that the weather matched my melancholy and thought I would just duck into a side shop until the downpour ceased, then continue by foot to my destination.

As I was standing in the shop, I was noticing a small child in the store with her mother, the shopkeeper, and was despondently pondering how different the culture was here. Still looking downward, I noticed a woman had stopped just inside the door and saw that she had navy blue flowery pants just like Alicia had and again I felt like crying with worry. At that moment, I looked up and it was Alicia! I screamed in disbelief: "Alicia!" "Mom!" "What are *you* doing here?" we screamed in unison. We both could not believe our eyes! She thought I was already in Tobago. She *had* been on the plane and I had obviously missed her. To fill time before the plane left for Tobago she had decided to take the afternoon to see Old Town. What was incredible to both of us is that she had just stopped there to get out her sweater because of the rain. She was heading back from *Parque de la Palomas* to sit in a market square and have coffee. To really appreciate the magnitude of this event is to know how large Old Town is and to know that there are literally hundreds of little shops up and down each street. We both felt that the only explanation was that divine intervention was at work.

In retrospect, I noticed that I was feeling out of my element—in a state of not-knowing—and following my impulses moment to moment. Also, I just had surrendered Alicia to her "angel" and asked that she be protected, knowing that she had traveled extensively, and

29

though there was absolutely nothing I could do, I hoped to see her that evening at the airport as we departed for Tobago. The remainder of the trip in Tobago was filled with synchronicities that seemed to occur only after each moment of surrender. It was not surrender in the sense of trusting that all would be well, but more of an "okay, I give in." Surrendering was not my forte, not in any sense of the word, and it felt very frustrating for me to be in the situation of group facilitator, with a defined agenda, and not to be able to keep on task. Each time I came up against my own ego task-oriented self, I had to let go, and hope we could manage something else out of it. I found that it was after this moment of surrender that synchronistic or oracular experiences would occur. These threshold experiences became commonplace because I was able to let go of all time-oriented, task-oriented ways of being and adopted the prolific "Tobagan" approach of "No problem!" I heard this so much it sounded like a daily mantra, and actually made me feel joyful each and every time I heard it. I finally learned what it meant to surrender to a larger field or source that seemed to operate outside my control.

It seems to me that the people of Tobago live in a perpetual state of oracular consciousness. A colleague and mentor, Dianne Skafte, who wrote *Listening to the Oracle,* states that oracular consciousness is a shifting of our awareness that allows us to listen for messages or allows images to speak to us from the world psyche. The people of Tobago seem to live life from this state and it is a part of their daily being. It is not thought about, in the same way that we Westerners live with our habits of thought and patterns of perception blinded by an ego-driven, task-minded orientation. We do not see our habitual thought processes objectively because we do not understand the paradigm we are living in until it is shifting to a newer paradigm. We do not recognize the significance of a new paradigm until the old one has died. However, because it appears that we are now examining the nature of ego consciousness, we may be in this death transition. I believe we Westerners sorely need a paradigm shift that can fully allow for oracular consciousness and our innate creative response.

Fear is a bedside fellow of the ego. Living outside of fear, or in the landscape of the oracular consciousness is an invitation to synchronicity in your life. Thich Nhat Hanh, a Tibetan monk and author of *The Miracle of Mindfulness*, refers to keeping your consciousness alive to the present reality, which he calls mindfulness. Mindfulness also invites the archetype of the "Fool" into our reality. The Fool steps forward on his path of life out of curiosity and trust. The Fool is open to the oracular/synchronistic events, tending to that which is happening inside and outside, being present now in both.

I have found that I can easily enter this place where time stops, known as Kairos time, when involved in painting, clay, gardening, writing. In this creative place, it seems as if a third thing arises and meets the creator. An energy flows between the doing and the being. It is as if my hands are being directed from another source and the clay forms itself, the paint paints a painting, the story writes the story, and plant spirits guide me in the garden in an effortless dance as if in a waking dream,

A colleague of mine who journeyed with me to Tobago met a man named Alex who was known as a "seer." She went to see Alex one day for a reading. Alex lives on a hilltop and has no telephone or television. She wondered how to find out if he was home. Her driver told her that Alex usually tunes in every day to ask whether or not to expect a visitor, so usually he "knows." Sure enough Alex was there and was expecting her. Earlier in the day he was instructed by his inner knowing or guidance to prepare an herb, and put it in a bag, which of course he did. When my friend arrived she spoke to Alex about her family and, "by the way," she asked, "might he recommend an herb for sleep?" He laughed and told her he had it already prepared as he was instructed to do so earlier and now he knew whom it was for! My friend was perplexed. She asked him how he knew? He told her that her "celestial being" had come and conversed with his "celestial being" preparing the way for her to come! This account invites me to wonder if indeed there was divine guidance behind following my impulses in San Juan: to leave the cab when I did, for the fortuitous downpour, and the choice of the street upon which I proceeded out of so many. Could there be another factor operating here that we have yet to explore?

The Universal Energy Field

Have you ever wondered how these "holes" in time or synchronistic windows open up? *How* do they get linked in the collective unconscious in the first place?

In psychology, there is a concept known as the interactive field. In therapeutic touch and other hands-on healing modalities there is a concept known as the universal energy field, or the universal web. In physics it is known as the *quantum field* or *psi-field*. These concepts are really not very different from the other. All of them embrace the idea of a subtle field that exists in the surround of all living things. In the previous story, Alex must have had access to information given to him through the universal field. He said that his "celestial being" gave him the information he needed for my friend. It was through some sort of portal in the fabric of time that his celestial helper contacted him and he was able to receive the information. Certainly, Alicia and I felt that we were divinely guided to the exact spot at exactly the right moment to "accidentally" find each other. Perhaps synchronicities are orchestrated by winged helpers who navigate the highways in the universal web of energy, the universal field. The intersections become portals where synchronicity abounds in the unified web.

Jung referred to this web as a *Unitarian Reality*. Jung felt there was a correspondence or at least a parallel, between the work of the new physics and his own research in depth psychology. In the latter 1920s, he began formulating his theory of acausal relationships, which he named synchronicity. According to Jean Shinoda Bolen, "He theorized that people as well as all animate and inanimate objects are linked through a collective unconscious. Just as modern atomic physics acknowledges that the researcher affects whatever he or she studies at the particle level, Jung suggested that the psyche of the observing person interacts in the moment with the events of the outside world."[6]

Jung was never satisfactorily able to link his ideas of synchronicity with physics and often suffered ridicule from the scientific community while studying these curiosities of the psyche. He defined synchronicity as a simultaneous and meaningful occurrence of certain psychic states with one or more external events.[7] What separates a coincidence from a synchronicistic experience is the word "meaningful." A coincidence does not have the sense of the divine at work, a sense of the sacred. A chance meeting of someone you know and were just thinking of may be simply a coincidence.

Jung stressed the point that since the physical and the psychic realms coincide within the synchronistic event, there must be somewhere or somehow a Unitarian reality—one reality of the physical and psychic realms to which he gave the Latin expression *unus mundus*, the one world, a concept that already existed in the minds of some medieval philosophers.[8] A friend and colleague of Jung, Maria-Louise von Franz, studied Chinese concepts of time and found that they have two aspects or ideas of time. One is timeless time or eternity, and the other is cyclic time superimposed on timeless time. This timeless time or synchronistic thinking she calls "thinking in fields."[9] This kind of time is sometimes referred to as *Kairos* time, named after the god of lucky coincidence, as opposed to cyclic time, named after the god, Chronos.

The ancient Chinese book of oracles, the *I Ching*, was based in a mathematical pattern that revealed the underlying structure of the universe. Jung thought that these numerical templates carry archetypal imprints that are revealed when the coins are thrown and the answer to a person's question becomes synchronized with the universal clock in that moment in time. As a result of his study of this ancient text and friendship with Richard Wilhelm, Jung began to formulate his ideas on synchronicity.

Synchronicity is literally like a hole in the fabric of "reality," and when it touches our consciousness it feels orchestrated by events behind the veil of time. They are transformative events that literally change us by our merging with the unified web that is made up of the subtle energy fields in the universal web of energy.

Imagine a lacy filament or web covering the planet and like in a three-dimensional holograph, there are converging points that illuminate the experience of oracular and synchronistic moments. These moments feel unworldly, timeless, and magical. It is like stepping into a portal where the mundane world—for at least a few moments—ceases to exist.

As we will see in the next chapter, the nature of the universal field involves a spectrum of energy that vibrates at multidimensional levels. It is like the subtle body of the human field, which also contains many levels and are also experienced through a shifting of consciousness. The levels are templates that hold energy, and consciousness. Energy and consciousness seem to be two terms often used synonymously. Yet, they are quite different in actuality. I cannot explain it any better than Woodhouse, who says, "*energy* and *consciousness* are the two most frequently encountered terms in New Paradigm discussions of the nature of reality. Thus we hear of the play of consciousness, the power of consciousness, and transcendental states of consciousness, along with energy fields, systems of energy, and healing energy, to mention a few."[10] He proposed the view that consciousness is the seat of meaningful or intelligent patterns of information that are expressed energetically over space and time. "Consciousness is thus a broader category not reducible to information or to energy."[11] Numinous moments (synchronistic events) are only a few of the threshold experiences that, when brushed up against, feel like sacred moments outside of the veil of time.

Chapter Two

Multiplicity, Liminality, and Inner Landscapes of the Soul

To Jung the imaginal soul is the "mother of all possibilities" joining together the inner and the outer worlds in a living union. Indeed the soul has all the earmarks of the Hindu Maya-Shakti – the creative energy of Brahman, the life-giving daemon who entangles man's consciousness with the world, conjuring up a delusory world by her dancing.

-Robert Avens Imagination is Reality

The Imaginal Realm

It is important to make a distinction between the imaginal and the imaginary. They are not at all the same thing. The imaginary or the imagination has been given a negative slant in our culture. It has been devalued and seen as "not real," therefore not factual nor objective in its reality. Since the advent of Descartes and the scientific worldview, the imagination has been assigned to the province of the child. Yet, I want to make it clear that the imaginal realm is not the imagination "reincarnated." The imagination, in fact, becomes the *key* that permits us into the imaginal realm. It is through the faculty of the imagination, what is called Active Imagination, that we are able to perceive intermediary realities and their sensory representations.[1] In fact, my hope is that by the end of this book, you will have a very real sense of this realm, with its multiple dimensions, and also various ways in which they are accessed.

There is a dimension or realm that exists between the physical realm and spiritual realms. It is made of vibrational bands that you can visit through altered states, which are referred to as the *mundus imaginalis*, the world of the imaginal. When Ibn'Arabi referred to this imaginal realm, he was speaking of an intermediate dimension, which functions as a third region, being neither of matter nor of spirit. He described it as a subtle realm, real in itself, which like a portal, makes it possible for all universes to make contact with the other.

This world is real and objective and is consistent and subsists as the intelligible and sensible world; it is an intermediate universe "where the spiritual takes the body and the body becomes the spiritual."[2] It is the place where archetypes are experienced, visions occur and where apparitions live. It is perhaps where the astral level of the Earth lives and is spoken of in theosophical philosophy, or in studies of the divine.

One way of entering the imaginal realm is through active imagination. Active imagination is a term most generally thought of as Jungian and in fact was borrowed by Jung from Ibn'Arabi's work. However, I believe active imagination is only one of the keys that admits us into the portals of imaginal realms. Certainly, active imagination, which I will discuss more thoroughly in Chapter Five, is an altered state and it is through altered states that we move into and through thresholds. But there are many kinds of altered states, and just as many ways to access them. When portals open or are felt through altered states, numinosity occurs, synchronistic events take place, and sentient beings become visible.

The Collective Unconscious

Jung was truly a visionary; writing during a time when the emphasis on a mechanistic world embedded in Cartesian thought left no room for the creative and spiritual nature of the psyche. Today, the idea of the collective unconscious may not seem so radical as it did when Jung introduced the concept, a time when the collective paradigm was still very entrenched in the calculated processes of scientific thought.

From his psychiatric work in a mental hospital, Jung began to see the unconscious as a wellspring of cultural and spiritual activity, which included ancestral memory. Jung called this the collective unconscious. The collective unconscious is like a human unconscious psychic matrix. Like James, Jung speaks to the "remarkable effects" of the unconscious contents as well as stating that once unconscious contents are activated, or have made themselves felt, they possess a specific energy that enables them to manifest everywhere. In a moment, I will give you some examples of this.

The collective unconscious, sometimes referred to as the objective psyche, has a deeper substrate that is referred to as the "psychoid." In this place, your personal psyche and world psyche's boundaries are thin. It is the place where subjective and objective states blend into one, where matter and spirit are no longer differentiated. This is a dimension of Ibn' Arabi's imaginal realm. Most recently, this blending—or bleeding—of the world psyche made itself known in my life as well as in the life of my clients. Sadly, as I write this, the United States has just endured one of the most horrific losses of death and destruction at the hands of terrorists who struck down The World Trade Center and the Pentagon. In separate sessions the week prior to this event, I had three people who came in telling me their dreams of being in foreign countries while trying to escape terrorists! All three of these people said to me that they were having odd dreams that did not feel like dreams they usually had. One woman said she was in some place "like Afghanistan," and was being held hostage there. The other two had dreams saying they were in an "Islamic country" and were trying to escape, while feeling threatened by terrorists. None of these people had ever been to these countries nor did they have any reason in their personal lives to have had these kinds of frightening dreams. It was only after September 11, 2001 did we understand that the world psyche (soul of the world) had impacted their dream life.

This is a perfect example of the collective unconscious at work. At that same time, many movies had been made in which The World Trade Center was being bombed or implicated. These movies were not released because the events in the movies were too uncannily close to the actual event. Once again it is not pure coincidence, but rather a deeper knowing that arises from the substrates of a world psyche where all events are accessible in a timeless vacuum.

Jung discovered the collective unconscious by finding common themes among his schizophrenic patients. He found that often they would speak to him of visions, and the themes in their artwork began to have common features among them. Jung further discovered that their drawings were similar to the art seen in his studies in alchemy. It was out of these correlations he formulated his theory of archetypes that reside in this layer of the collective psyche. Many images common to humankind are revealed through dreams and art in the form of archetypes. Within the confines of a psychiatric hospital, Jung found that archetypal motifs were universal to all human psyches throughout the world!

Archetypes

Archetypes are psychic blueprints that govern the expression of symbolic images found throughout human history. We cannot know an archetype directly; only through its energetic expression in symbols do we know of their presence. An example of this phenomenon is in children's art seen across the world. Rhoda Kellogg, in her research of cross-cultural children's art, noticed that children begin making scribbles that correspond to their age, and that the development of these scribbles to human form can be seen across the boundaries of culture and time. She discovered that the scribbles develop into "suns" or mandalas, then into human form. Kellogg states that the "Mandala and the sun appear to provide the stimulus for the child's first drawings of a Human."[3] The mandala is an example of an ancient symbol of wholeness found throughout history and in every culture. It is an archetype or universal symbol, which is inherent in the human psyche, yet exists *a priori* to it. Like the stars that exist in the skies before our birth and will exist after our death, archetypes are guiding soul prints that manifest to mediate between our conscious mind and the collective unconscious.

In my work as a Jungian Sandplay therapist, this same premise holds true. Adults and children select small miniatures and place them in a sandtray. These miniatures represent archetypal symbology that mediates between the conscious mind and the unconscious realm. It provides a way to enter a liminal or threshold place that then allows for psychic expression and the internalization of its needs. Like in a dream, in imagery, in art, or in the sandtray, the psyche generates the images it needs for its wholeness and growth. This quest for wholeness takes people on a journey. It is often an initiatory experience that opens one deeper to soul knowing.

Children automatically understand the meaning of fairytales without questioning them. The images of the story hold universal meaning that children grasp at an unconscious level. The story often embodies an initiatory journey of the lessons in life, and the quest for wholeness. The situation of being lost in the wilderness or forest, for example, is present in many fairytales. This is a universal motif known to all mankind, the feeling of being lost. Many films are made with this basic archetype—or motif— embedded in the story. The Wise Old Man, The Crone, The Hero, Scapegoat, Trickster, Birth, Death, the Tree of Life, and the Journey are a few other archetypes and archetypal themes found in story and film.

Because it is difficult to describe archetypal experiences, I will give you another example of how an archetypal energy can manifest in one's life. A woman I had been working with who was raised Catholic began feeling attracted to the image of Kwan Yin, goddess of compassion, on my sandplay shelf. She had not ever noticed her before, yet suddenly she couldn't keep it out of her mind. She then began searching for a Kwan Yin in stores, as she wanted this goddess for her altar. Kwan Yin began appearing to my client in her dream life as well. In waking life, I believe this archetypal energy, or the urge to have Kwan Yin in her life, presented itself because she was working with compassion for herself and others in her therapeutic process.

Archetypes can only be known through the experience of them, either in psychic phenomena or somatic phenomena, or somewhere in between. It is not that they are either one or the other; actually archetypes hold the opposite polarities, for example in the "Mother" archetype, both the good fairy and the bad mother as seen in the witch are both part of the Mother archetype. Since we can only know an archetype through its various symbols, when we are embraced by an archetypal energy, the symbols become alive with meaning as did

39

Kwan Yin with my client. We fall in love with the symbol, we seek it out, we find that it appears everywhere in our life. However, it can work the opposite way as well.

Janice, a woman in one of my dream groups hated snakes, yet they kept appearing in her inner and outer life. She found them on the road, in and around her house, and on camping trips, as well as in her walks in nature. Her husband, being a naturalist, did not wish to kill the snakes, so captured them when they found them and placed them in a glass aquarium to let free later, but the aquarium was in her garage where Janice saw them every day. Janice came every month with a dream of snakes. In many of these dreams she had come face to face with them. In one memorable dream, she was hanging upside down in a cavern, eye to eye with a deadly snake. On the personal level, these snake dreams probably symbolized her fears. Yet on the archetypal level, they have many other meanings.

In some cultures, snakes are kept in the house for good luck. Because snakes shed their skin, they are seen as symbols of transformation, and because snakes live close to Earth and in the Earth, they are seen as guardians of the Earth Goddess. Snake energy is often related to the Kundalini, an energy residing at the tailbone, which once released, is said to snake up the spine and cause the person a shift in awareness. (This is a very brief and simplistic explanation of Kundalini energy. For more information, I direct you to Bonnie Greenwell's book, *Energies of Transformation*.) Sometimes, the outer world mirrors back the inner world. Whatever Snake wanted from Janice is still in incubation. I believe she will continue meeting Snake until she finds what it wants her to know. At the summer break from dream group, Janice decided to do some shamanic journeying to see if Snake would give her more information on the archetypal level of being.

Symbolic images are not just stored in the psyche somewhere to be released when the need arises. As we saw in the example of Snake in Janice's life, which manifested both in outer reality and in symbolic images in dreamtime, archetypal symbols occur in the interface between individual and environment, through the interaction of archetypes with perceptions and experiences. It is also a matrix of energy that has the ability to attract or repel. Like Janice, any time we are in a strong reaction to something or someone, we are in the grip of an unconscious projection generated by an archetypal pull.

Contact with an archetypal energy has power to bring change into our lives. A friend of mine had been thinking a lot about death. After buying a used car, he had the odd feeling that someone had died in it. The next day, as he was sitting in this vehicle near sundown, an owl flew through the window and onto the front seat! My friend became quite upset, as the owl seemed disoriented was unable to get out of the car. Finally, the owl freed itself, but the incident was quite unsettling for my friend because he thought of the owl as an omen of death. Native American tradition holds the owl as a harbinger of great, and lasting change, death being only one kind of transformation. It seems to me that the archetype of change and transition held by the symbol of Owl magnetically attracted the living owl to my friend. This synchronistic event may have been the harbinger of his decision to retire after many years in his profession, presenting a very dramatic change and life transformation for him.

How does an archetypal energy manifest like this in waking life? The archetype is said to have a "field" effect; or the power to constellate something—a "magnetic" tendency to stimulate and draw to itself events that correspond to it—to ensure that inner predispositions and outer events belong together due to the structure of our inner life and our outer relationships mirroring each other.[4] Tapping into this realm elicits the energetic source and creative ground of our being. It also constellates events in the outer world as a mirror and guide for our inner world, and journey on the path to Self. Although not all outer world events and situations are archetypal, it may still be a wonderful practice to see life as a mirror for inner processes. If you have never thought about outer world events in these ways, I suggest a small exercise of looking up the meaning of symbols as you encounter them in daily life or dream life. As a beginning, many people like the medicine cards for looking up the archetypal meaning of animals they come across in waking life.

Archetypal Fields

Archetypal fields are what orchestrate synchronistic events. Its magnetic qualities are a key to understanding the electric sensation that takes place when entering a threshold state. The archetypal field is unique from other fields due to its nonlocality. Many of the effects of fields occurring in three-dimensional matter can be measured, such as electromagnetic fields. Archetypal fields, on the other hand, appear to function nonlocally as they are not space-time dependent and scientists believe that archetypal fields emit specific archetypal frequencies, which impact us whether we know it or not.[5] In other words, some fields can be measured and obey the laws of the three-dimensional world. Yet other fields, such as archetypal fields, move beyond the veil of "Chronos" or linear time. When a person is in the grip of an archetypal field, he has experiences that seem to magically correspond with what is in his awareness of it.

I remember a woman who came to a workshop I was leading in which I guided people in an interactive imagery exercise. They were to go to a sacred garden or outdoor place to meet an inner guide. This woman saw an image of a goddess very specifically coming out of a tree. The next day, she purchased a magazine and the feature article was about the goddess Artemis. As she opened the page, she saw the exact image she had seen the day before in her imagery. It was a depiction of the goddess Artemis. She was very surprised and excited to find this image. The synchronistic meeting of this goddess will surely bring new meaning to her life.

Any time we have been energized by an archetype we enter its field effect, an interactive field in the imaginal zones. Being under the influence of an archetypal field is a very real, lived experience. Even though you may not be conscious of what archetypal patterns live in the backdrop of your life, you will still be under their influence. Archetypal patterns are what astrologers use to look at charts. These universal themes are the matrix of all life. To experience and recognize these archetypal fields, we may use perceptual organs outside of the five senses. Altered states though imagery, dreams, or by looking objectively at the story of your life are ways to recognize the archetypal theme you may have been living or that has been living you. Understanding these motifs in fairytales or through movies is another way to see into the archetypal arena in which you have been influenced by or living.

Perhaps this is the field that visionaries tap into, or the realm where gods and goddesses abide and where myths and fairytales are birthed. When we are in contact with an archetypal field, the field itself brings matter and psyche together in synchronistic events. I notice a sensory experience when I have crossed this threshold into an activated or archetypal field. I always get chills on the right hand side of my body. You may notice a different sensory experience when crossing a threshold into these liminal realms where archetypal patterns and universal energy fields abound.

What archetypal energy is exerting influence in your life? Have you been living the myth of the Hero, or Psyche and Eros, or perhaps Dorothy in the Wizard of Oz? Many myths and stories impart these same challenges, like those of Dorothy who finds that after facing many challenges she had the knowledge she needed all along to return home; home being a symbol of the Self. I had a professor who once said that we are all living a myth, knowing which one is what gives our lives richness, depth and meaning. Once you recognize the archetypal journey you have been living, you can choose consciously to change the course of your life, a choice Sophocles' King Oedipus didn't have.

Dreams in the Liminal World

Dreams are another kind of threshold in liminal time in which we enter nightly. Dreams are a nightly portal into our own personal unconscious or through which the world psyche contacts us. Many indigenous cultures believe that we are always in dreamtime, even when we are so-called awake. As we look around the globe, it becomes clear that our Western ideas of what is real and not real is guided by the culture we live in. Many cultures define reality differently than the Western culture, and similarly, how a culture values dreams and the interpretation of them is linked to the culture's beliefs.[6]

43

Dreams like the one in the example above of the woman who began to dream of snakes found that Snake appeared in "waking" life as well are seen in many cultures as one reality. In other words, all waking time is dreamtime. Consider this example of another woman who was scheduled to do a presentation on the turtle as an archetype in one of my classes. The day of the presentation she said she had to stop her car to let a large land tortoise cross the road. Several minutes later while stopped in traffic, she saw that a man in the car next to her had a large turtle tattooed on his arm. She commented through the open window that she was on her way to do a turtle presentation and he launched into his love of turtles and turtle stories in his life. My Western education allows me to understand how these "coincidences" are perfect examples of how, when an archetypal field is constellated, the outer world manifests what we are working on psychically. These instances feel like threshold experiences, which alert a person to the noetics of a universe that exists beyond the mundane world.

Perhaps another cultural view would see Snake and Turtle as part of dreamtime or live embodiments of spirit totems guiding the dreamer through an initiation, or which have come to give the dreamer powerful medicine. To indigenous peoples, dreamscapes are real places in the physical world, and are not divided between waking time and dreaming time. Elders and shamen are known to have the power to affect cure through dreams by entering the dream world through trance states, to recover lost souls, fight evil spirits, and contact ancestors on behalf of the dreamer.[7]

Dreams have played an important role throughout history. In Biblical times dreams were seen as prophetic. In Egypt dreams were seen as revelations from the gods or as visions for future events. Dreams were taken seriously by the Pharaoh and were given primacy in decisions of rulership over the land. Dreams were seen as revelations from the gods or as visions for future events.

Dreams were of such vital import that in ancient Greece 410 dream temples were dedicated to Aesclepius, the Greek God of medicine. The practice of dream incubation thrived for a thousand years up until the 15th century.

> Anyone was welcome free of charge, except those who
> were dying and pregnant women (because they were

not sick). Healing was promoted: sanctuaries included priests, attendants, massage therapists, and other skilled practitioners to foster healing and preparation. After baths, fasting, ritual and prayer, patients descended into a lower chamber (close to the ground) to sleep on goat's skins and awaited a dream visitation from Aesclepius or other Gods and Goddesses. These persons slept in the temples until a dream revealed the origin of illness as well as the suggested treatment. As a matter of fact, thousands of pilgrims received miraculous cures in this way.[8]

Personal and practical use of dreams continued up through the Middle Ages. In the Medieval ages, Cabalists practiced dream incubation regularly, feeling that dreams came from divine inspiration. By the 3rd century A.D., dreams began to fall out of favor when St. Jerome discouraged "pagan" incubation practices. By the 19th century, dreams were beginning to be seen from psychological perspectives. Heinrich von Schubert Gotthiff (1780–1860) wrote "dreams are a universal language of symbols that are the same for all people in all places and times."[9]

Later, Freud made famous the notion that dreams are "royal roads to the unconscious." No longer having the role as messengers between the gods and humanity, dreams became the messenger between the ego and the unconscious. By the time Freud was writing about dreams, dreams were seen as manifestations of pathological states. Jung, then a student of Freud, began to see dreams differently than Freud. This ultimately led to a branch of psychology that brought validity back to dream life. Unlike Freud, Jung felt that the meanings of dreams were not disguised, repressed wishes, but were a direct source into a well of knowledge that went beyond the personal confines of the psyche. Borrowing a phrase from the Talmud, Jung said, "An uninterpreted dream is like a letter from God unopened." Once again dreams found their way back to the realm of the divine.

Exercise #1

Dream Recall

Remembering your dreams is not always easy to do. It takes practice. Upon waking in the morning, try to stay in the position you were in while dreaming. Ask yourself, what was I just dreaming? To remember your dreams it is important not to jump up or be awakened by the alarm. Before going to sleep, set a conscious intention that you will remember your dreams. This is a big signal to the unconscious that is has work to do in the night. Putting a journal next to our bed anchors this intention. If you awaken in the middle of the night, write down a few words from the dream. This is often enough to bring total recall in the morning. Do not think, "Oh, I will remember this in the morning." Chances are that you won't. Some people prefer a tape recorder to use to record a few words in the middle of the night. Often, people are completely surprised to find that they recorded a dream in the middle of the night, with no recall of doing so! With a few nights of setting the intention, your dream psyche will know you are serious and you will begin to feel successful. I find that the more dreams I write down, the more I remember.

* * *

In Chapters Five and Seven I will give you more examples and tips to working with your personal dreams as important inner resources and guidance.

Sacred Mind and Oracular Consciousness

Perhaps it is not we who dream the dream. Perhaps, it is the universe dreaming us, which is what we then experience. Ironically, through quantum physics, science may take us back to what the indigenous peoples have known all along: that the Earth is conscious, not us. Stephen Aisenstat, a prominent dream tender, asks us to notice how we are often aware of ourselves as an integral part of a dream. Notice that there is an aware ego in the dream and we are experiencing ourselves as that ego part. Aisenstat asks, if we are in the dream, then who is it that is dreaming the dream (*Personal Communication*)? Perhaps it is the Sacred Mind dreaming the dream and we are simply one of its dream embodiments.

Author Christopher Bache in his book, *Dark Night, Early Dawn: Steps to a Deep Ecology of the Mind*, speaks of Sacred Mind, referring to the transpersonal, or universal mind in which a numinous sense of the wholeness of reality is experienced. Bache says to experience Sacred Mind even briefly profoundly shifts one's sense of identity because it gives you an entirely new reference point from which to experience the life process. Sacred Mind reaches us through non-ordinary states of consciousness. Eastern, mystical, and indigenous traditions have had this insight for thousands of years. People cross-culturally have experienced it through meditation practices, sacred medicine, psychedelics, dreams, and synchronicities, just to name a few ways of entering the portals where the numinous lives and Sacred Mind can be experienced.

Bache has explored the sacred mind through what he calls "psychedelic" states of mind. He is referring more to "mind opening states" rather than the use of ingested chemical states.[10] Bache has for many years studied the nature of the psyche through Stan Grof's model of holotropic breathwork, and shares with the reader Bache's personal transcriptions of reaching transpersonal and transformative states therein. Bache feels strongly that we, as a species need to let go of our "atomistic thinking" and replace it with the knowledge that we are all interrelated by an integral psychic web that questions the illusion of ego boundaries. In one of his transcripts from a session he gives us a beautiful example of the experience of Sacred Mind:

> The unified field underlying physical existence completely dissolved all boundaries. As I moved deeper into it, all borders fell away; all appearances of division were ultimately illusory. No boundaries between incarnations, between human beings, between species, even between matter and spirit. The world of

individuated existence was not collapsing into an amorphous mass, as it might sound, but rather was revealing itself to be an exquisitely diversified manifestation of a single entity.[11]

Another way that the universal mind contacts us in the imaginal realm is through oracular consciousness. Rather than through imagery coming in contact with us, this threshold experience announces itself through its clairaudient nature. "Oracles fulfill a profound need in spiritual life. We long to be addressed in an intimate, helpful way by something wiser than ourselves. We yearn to feel our connection with the larger matrix of existence," says Dianne Skafte, author of *Listening to the Oracle*. Skafte defines an oracle by its experience, "To receive an oracle is to receive guidance, knowledge, or illumination from a mysterious source beyond the personal self."[12] Skafte states that nearly anything may serve as a channel for oracles, and lists dreams, inspired trance states, spontaneous encounters with the natural world, inquiry through divination, and revelation through music and art are a few of the ways in which you may experience an oracular event. When in the presence of an oracle, states Skafte, "one experiences the atmosphere in the room changing, a feeling of presence and portent fills the surround, all time stops, and it as if something larger than the self steps in."[12] Again a sense of the holy enters, and the numinous experience forever remains fresh in our psyches.

For me, Sacred Mind is the deep connection to Earth and all her sentient beings. I choose to see the world full of ensouled beings that wish to make contact with us. Perhaps Mother Earth or Gaia's Sacred Mind ushered in Turtle and Snake into my clients' field to remind them of Her Presence. Gaia is an ancient name given to the goddess of the Earth. For some, dreams and oracular events such as these are the portals through which Gaia can reach us, make contact, and remind us of our soul connection with her. It is as if Sacred Mind orchestrates a grand scheme behind the illusory veil of the every day world. I believe we must find a way to reconcile our thinking about the world and our selves before we wear out our welcome with our gracious hostess.

In *Spell of the Sensuous*, David Abram refers to the experiences he had in Indonesia and Nepal that shifted the focus of his research. He discovered that nonhuman nature can be perceived and experienced with far more intensity and nuance than is generally acknowledged in the West.[13] "For almost all oral cultures, the enveloping and sensuous earth remains the dwelling place of both the living and the dead. The body—whether human or otherwise—is not yet a mechanical object in such cultures, but is a magical entity, the mind's own sensuous aspect, and at death the body's decomposition into soil, worms, and dust can only signify the gradual reintegration of one's ancestors and elder into the living landscape, from which all, too are born."[14]

Abram is essentially an eco-psychologist, who sees the world as animated—an ensouled world—and wishes to awaken the Western psyche to this knowing. Unlike the archetypal psychologist's world, Abram enters an intermediate realm where all sentient beings have a literalized persona. Western culture seems to me to invalidate the autonomy of the ancestors or sentient beings. In archetypal and Jungian psychology the ancestors are relegated to the multiplicity of the psyche, and it stops short of offering validity to their ontological presence. In other words, do the ancestors have a reality of their own, rather than being an idea born out of our psychology?

Jung seemed to wrestle with this question in some of his writing. Jung used active imagination as a technique to confront the unconscious contents of the psyche. Active imagination is a way that you begin to find a dialogue with the interior contents of the psyche residing in the unconscious, both personal and collective. During these kinds of confrontations, these images and beings begin to have a life of their own. They begin to speak and have things to say. They do not change form as sometimes happens in guided imageries or as in shamanic travels. As an illustration of this, Jung met a being that called himself "Philemon" in the active imagination process. Jung confessed that much of his writing came through his daily dialogues with Philemon. I will speak more of Philemon as an inner resource and "Otherworld" being in Chapter Five. Jung thought that we couldn't truly know ourselves until we have learned to know the autonomous, albeit unconscious parts of the psyche. These parts often have conflictual desires from the waking ego, and drives that may be totally foreign to the ego self. The shadow parts, or split-off parts, which are projected onto others, reside in the unconscious. Through active imagination and dream process, we can learn who and what these aspects of our self are about. One of the tenants of the process in confronting these parts is that one must retain the ego's perspective. Jung differentiated this "active" process from that of a passive process, such as guided imagery, or fantasy, in which the image can change forms. Although Jung used active imagination to confront the "complexes" (traumatic core issues) within the personal unconscious, he did not write about active imagination as a portal into the realms of other worlds. However, for Ibn' Arabi, active imagination was the key to entering the sacred domains in the imaginal world.

Psyche or Spirit?

Jung asked a tantalizing question, "Does the psyche in general—that is, the spirit, or the unconscious— arise in us; or is the psyche actually outside us in the form of arbitrary powers with intentions of their own, and does it gradually come to take its place within us in the course of psychic development? Were dissociated psychic contents ever parts of the psyches of individuals, or were they rather from the beginning psychic entities existing in themselves according to the primitive view as ghosts, ancestral spirits and the like?"[15] In other words, we can ask, was Philemon a part of Jung's psyche or did he live as an Otherworld being wherein active imagination was the portal through which they made contact? Perhaps we will never know the answer to this question, and perhaps the answer is not what is important. What is important is that we stay open to our lived experiences, while keeping alive the ability to invite threshold experiences into our lives.

I have had a very vivid experience of being contacted by an Otherworld being in a session with a client who lost his fiancé suddenly the week before they were to be married. I had heard about her death from several other clients who knew her, but had never met her myself. I was not surprised when her fiancé, "John" called soon after her death for an appointment to deal with his grief. During his appointment the next week, I began to feel the slightly electrified sense that I have when I have moved into the threshold of a field. As John was telling me of her and his love for her, I began to get the chills, and standing to the right of me Belinda suddenly "appeared."

I could see her clearly, her height, her hair color, her energy. She was extremely distraught, and she began pacing the room. At one point, she leaned over me and fairly shouted for me to tell him that "she loved him and was sorry."

At this point, I was very distraught myself, and frankly, did not know how to proceed. I did not want to tell John that I could see her there, although I asked him to describe her to me. Of course, he described her exactly as I was seeing her. I had never seen Belinda prior to this, nor had I seen her picture. I suppose I could have been reading his mind, but she seemed to be acting autonomously. At one point, she sat next to him, and wanted to make contact with him. It was like a scene in a movie, when two people try to touch each other through a glass partition in a prison. It was a very emotional experience for me—and uncomfortable.

I did *not* want our sessions to become a sort of channeling, and further, I did *not* want to do psychic work. I wanted to help my client with his grief. Finally, I began saying to John, "I am sure if she were here, she would want you to know . . ." this seemed to appease them both. Belinda wanted me to tell him to read a book—I kept hearing, *The Tibetan Book of the Living and Dying*. Because this was our first session, I had no idea if he would receive this well or not. But trusting what I was hearing, I asked John if he knew of this book. He said, "Oh, my Gosh, I just pulled that book off her shelf last night, but didn't open it."

John felt that Belinda was his true love, and deeply grieved her loss. He had never felt this much love for any one else in his 39 years of life. He told me that he felt that he had been with her for "many lifetimes." At one point, I took him into a "holographic regression" (see Chapter Four) to uncover any other lives he might have lived out with her. In one life, he saw that they were of a very different class. He worked in a kitchen of sorts and she would come in occasionally and visit with him. He saw that she eventually married someone else, and felt extremely bereft at losing her. In a Greek life, he was able to experience having her throughout his life, both of them living to old age. This was very gratifying for him, and seemed to give him some support through his grief. John had had several family losses the year before his fiancé's death, and he told me that he often thought of joining Belinda through the act of suicide.

John was desperate to have the opportunity to contact her one more time since her sudden death left him without any way to have closure, so he decided to try to reach her through a well-known psychic who had come to the area. In this session with her, the psychic was able to make contact with Belinda. John reported to me that Belinda could see his intention to join her and she told him that even if he came over, he would not be with her! He was taken aback when she said that. She told him she had many things she had to do and, further, that they were at different levels of "soul experience." John told me that hearing this was the only thing that kept him here. I was surprised to hear this as well as I also had assumed that he could be with her if he were to cross the threshold. Although difficult to describe, this experience had a subtle, but different energetic "feel" than some of the other threshold experiences that I have had.

I believe that the bandwidths of energy in the levels of the imaginal can be tapped in threshold states. For me, the levels of the imaginal field, wherein entities live, seem to have phenomenological differences in the way they are experienced. The field is charged with a signature of its own, like the octaves on a piano, each with its own resonance. These ideas and experiences go beyond the field of psychology. Psychology has left me without tools toward understanding the dynamics of the imaginal realms and how to interface with them in psychological settings. Nevertheless, these experiences have led me to research the outer regions of the mind, and inner landscapes of the soul.

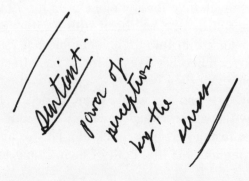

Chapter Three

Blurring Boundaries

In a particular city all the inhabitants were blind. One day the king of the realm came to visit on a mighty elephant and all the people ran in the hope to see the elephant. But since they were blind, they could only grope sightlessly and touch whichever part they could reach with their hands. Yet each thought that he knew something because he would feel a part. Afterwards they were eager to share their discovery with their fellow citizens who wished to learn the "truth" about the elephant.

One man who happened to have touched the ear said that an elephant was a large, rough thing, wide and broad, like a rug.

The one who had felt the trunk protested that he had the real facts: it is like a straight and hollow pipe, awful and destructive. The one who had felt its legs said: It is mighty and firm like a pillar.

Each had perceived a part only; no one could realize that which is beyond sensual capacity.

-Retold, from Idries Shah, Tales of the Dervishes

Science or Science Fiction?

This Sufi story seems to be an apt metaphor for my experience in archiving the scientific realm with regard to the universal field, especially in the world of microphysics or quantum physics. Examining the field vis-à-vis the lens of physicists is a daunting enterprise, since it seems that each has its favored theory or paradigm of the nature of the universe. If you will allow me to go into the scientific world, I will give you as simple an understanding as possible of how threshold experiences are supported in the world by quantum physics. In this chapter, I want to look at the notion of interactive fields in nature which demonstrate how energy works as a vibratory pattern that may be accessed through our conscious intention. These interactive fields become symbolic "portals" through which threshold experiences are possible because of the universal web of energy that surrounds all life. These webs are like fields that become highways or bandwidths of frequency from which to travel on or in. Threshold states of consciousness are experienced when one enters the various frequencies through a shifting of consciousness.

This chapter takes the reader on a scientific journey through the evolution of scientific paradigms that explores the dynamics of nature and ultimately consciousness. We will be looking at consciousness and energy as fields within the realms of micro science. We will see how science has discovered interactive fields in the universal web of energy. We will also be looking at the cosmology of the holographic universe as a model for how energy fields exist in both local and nonlocal ways. If you are not interested in knowing the whys and hows, or the "nuts and bolts" behind threshold experiences, I suggest skipping this chapter and moving directly to the next.

Paradigm Shifts

Thomas Kuhn first described the structure of paradigms in his classic book, *The Structure of Scientific Revolutions* in 1962. He pointed out that science proceeds by way of what he called paradigms. He said that a paradigm is not merely a concept; it is an actual practice, an injunction, a technique taken as an *exemplar* for generating data. Kuhn's point is that genuine scientific knowledge is grounded in paradigms, exemplars, and injunctions, which bring forth new data.[1] Kuhn stated that the scientist's method of questioning is usually shaped by the prevailing world image or scientific theory. Kuhn said that every now and then, a paradigm shift occurs, and the perspectives of science get smashed and scientists begin to look at things through a different lens.[2] This seems to be what is happening with the advent of quantum physics.

Mark Woodhouse, author of *Paradigm Wars: Worldviews for a New Age*, points out that in the last 60 years, the "Rising Culture" has taken a decidedly sharp turn toward a systems model and away from the materialist, reductionistic thinking of the Cartesian era. Woodhouse borrows this term from Fritjof Capra, referring to "all persons, trends, and cultural institutions whose actions and perspectives are informed by the New Paradigm dialogue and to some extent by New Age agendas."[3] This movement is widespread and has infiltrated many areas from medicine to metaphysics. For example, I have found that this movement enthusiastically embraced areas of lucid dreaming, brain physiology, energetic healing, and Eastern mysticism. Often this central model of holistic thinking is promoted to further support the nature of each of these theories.

As an archetypal happening, it seems that psyche has had enough of unintegrated parts science and yearns for a more integrated point of view. Although scientific materialism has been one of the most successful master paradigms of the last four hundred years, and has been deeply entrenched in the Western psyche, the unified, holistic model seems to be taking hold.[4]

This new paradigm embraces wholeness, balance, integration, and nonlocality. Out of this thrust is the notion of field theory in contemporary science and seems to be directly related to the interactive field in psychology. Interactive fields were born out of the discovery of quantum fields in physics. However, the interactive field in psychology deals with consciousness and the notion of fields in physics concerns energy—the two are related but are not interchangeable.

Constance S. Rodriguez, PhD

Competing Worldviews

Before reviewing the holographic paradigm and quantum physics, I want to lay a foundation for understanding the various scientific models by giving you a sort of map that situates the scientific paradigms in specific consciousness paradigms. I would also like you to have a sense of these competing worldviews so expediently outlined by Christian de Quincey in his article, "Consciousness, Truth, or Wisdom?" in *IONS, Noetic Sciences Review* (2000), in which he details the prevailing worldviews underlying these perspectives in the next section on quantum physics.

According to de Quincey, basically there are four worldviews that authors utilize. It is important to discern which viewpoint the author is holding as a premise to follow his or her ideas; and, more importantly, these worldviews explain why there are so many arguments over the nature of reality. As you read further in this chapter, I will point out which worldview an author is writing from. The four worldviews that dominate most writing are: dualism, materialism, idealism, and panpsychism. (de Quincey goes into much more detail regarding these worldviews in his book, *Radical Nature, 2002*).

De Quincey states in his article that the metaphysical view of dualism is that both mind and matter are real but separate. He says that the core problem is in the interaction of the two and that dualism requires a miracle to "explain" how "two utterly different and separate substances could ever interact." The next view de Quincey looks at is the materialistic view. He states that in this view, only matter is ultimately real and that here the core problem with this view is one of emergence, "materialism faces the insuperable problem of explaining how mind could emerge for mindless matter." He says, "For mind to emerge from matter, for consciousness to appear in the natural world, would require some kind of miraculous intervention."

The next worldview that de Quincy outlines is that of idealism. In this worldview, only the mind or consciousness is real. He states, "Idealism denies that the physical world has any reality of its own, and it asks us to believe that either all matter is an illusion (*maya*) or that matter emanates from pure mind or spirit." De Quincey points out that we are left with the pragmatic problem of how to live in the

56

world if we do not treat matter as real. In his words, "idealism asks us to reject the natural world as having any substantial reality in its own right."

The last worldview, according to de Quincey, is that of panpsychism. It holds that consciousness and matter are inseparable. De Quincey says that it penetrates all the way down, "so that even single cells, molecules, atoms, or electrons are bundles of sentient energy." This view takes the position that both mind and matter are real and natural and neither takes priority over the other.[5] *Sacred Portals* is written from the panpsychic viewpoint of reality and embraces the theory that all things have an ontological (the nature of being or reality) level of consciousness.

The first two models are straight out of the Cartesian/Newtonian paradigm that has dominated the past few hundred years. Jung devoted most of his writing to the problem of opposites and studied alchemy as an answer to the problem of duality. Idealism, seen more predominantly in New Age thinking, proposes that mind is all there is and is rooted in many religious traditions, more notably in Eastern traditions. On the other hand, "dualists assert that minds have different properties from bodies and are thus a different kind of thing,"[6] whereas panpsychism believes that they are only different in subtleties. Panpsychism may not only be a bridge where psyche and matter meet, but can also be thought to be fluid in its movement to and fro on the psyche/matter continuum. We will see in the evolution of microphysics how the physicists have struggled with these problems.

The scientists of these paradigms are arguing the nature of consciousness and matter. Woodhouse stated neither consciousness nor energy is reducible to the other, although each is reflected in the other. He goes on to say that many commentators use "energy" and "consciousness" interchangeably in certain contexts. Strictly speaking, however, they are not equivalent terms. To observe brain-wave energy on a monitor, for example, is not to observe a person's thoughts or feelings.[7] This paradox has continued to confound scientists who are hoping to find that matter supports that which is immeasurable, or a theory that resolves the problem.

What does comprise consciousness? Although I don't presume to know the answer to this perennial question, traditionally, consciousness is assumed to be either a nonphysical "ghost in the machine" or else the very same thing as our brain or a part of the "machine" itself. (The "ghost in the machine" refers to Arthur Koestler's auspicious book by that name. It asks the question of what it is that operates the mind, wherein Koestler uses the metaphor of the television set. This metaphor points out that although we see images in a television, they are not being produced by the television.) "Either consciousness is something other than the brain, as dualism holds, or it is identical with the biochemical processes that make up our brain and nervous system, as materialism holds. Either our minds interact with our bodies and can carry on (at least for a while) without our bodies (dualism), or the only interaction is between brains and bodies, and the death of the body *is* the end of the mind (materialism)."[8]

The mind-only view—idealism—as previously stated, does not differentiate mind and matter, but rather includes matter as part of the mind. The idealist position states that we cannot experience objectively, no matter how physical objects may seem. All objects are only various kinds of thoughts that can only be experienced through the mind. Victor Mansfield, a physicist who upholds the mind-only view, points out that this view does not eliminate the reality of the experience of nature. In contrast to de Quincey's view of idealism, Mansfield states that all experience is a "complex of images shimmering in the psyche and that it does not rob experience of any of its vividness. Stones are just as hard and heavy, pains and joys just as acute."[9]

Another example of the mind-only view originating out of Buddhist thought is that there cannot be a baby without its mother, or a tree without the Earth,[10] and we cannot not know these independent of the other. In other words, all things are interdependent on the other.

Quantum Leaps

At the turn of the 20th century, scientists discovered another way to see the world. It was through quantum physics, or microphysics that an unsettling phenomenon was observed. For science, the basis of the physical world was solid matter—indestructible units or building blocks called atoms. Then suddenly, a new discovery was made. Atoms were not solid but were composed of electrons, protons, and neutrons, which were unfathomably minute compared to an atom, which already were seen as mostly empty space.[11]

Basically, what researchers found was a paradox. Particles and waves never behaved in the same way even though experiments were set up in exactly the same manner. "Physics was forced to come to a nondualist acceptance of nature as subatomics baffled the physicists. Depending on how the experiment was set up, a subatomic entity may appear as a particle, or if looked at another way, it was a wave. Adding to the mystery, subatomic particles can jump from one orbit of an atom to another without touching the intervening space... Finally, when two particles in a certain state of relationship drift apart from one another in space—no matter how distantly apart...they are found to display a nonlocal connection; i.e., they have a relationship which cannot be explained or accounted for in terms of any force of interaction between them."[12]

Physicist and author, Fritz Capra, states that we owe our current state of understanding in quantum physics largely due to two men, Michael Faraday and Clerk Maxwell, a scientist and theorist, respectively, who made a major shift in the history of science when the forces in electric and magnetic fields became object of their studies. "They replaced the concept of a force by that of a force field, and in doing so they were the first to go beyond the Newtonian physics."[13] When Maxwell and Faraday created a current in a copper coil by moving a magnet near it that created a charge, they called it a "disturbance" or "condition." It is this condition in space that has the potential of producing a force that was called a field. Capra continues by stating the force concept was then "replaced by a subtler concept of a field that had its own reality and could be studied without any reference to material bodies. The culmination of this theory, called electrodynamics, was the realization that light is nothing but a rapidly alternating electromagnetic field traveling through space in the form of waves. Today we know that radio waves, light waves or X-rays, are all electromagnetic waves, oscillating electric and magnetic fields differing only in the frequency of their oscillation."[14]

At the turn of the 20th century, Albert Einstein revolutionized modern physics with a theory that also served to undermine the

Newtonian worldview: the theory of relativity and what is now called quantum theory, or the theory of atomic phenomena. In this famous theory of relativity, E=mc², space-time is not three-dimensional and time is not a separate entity. "Both are intimately connected and form a four-dimensional continuum, 'space-time'." Because of his discovery, now there is no such thing as "empty space" in the universe.[15]

As a result of Einstein's theory of relativity, a group of international physicists continued studying the laws of physics that Einstein introduced. The now-famous men in this group, Neils Bohr, Louis De Brogile, Erwin Schrodinger, Werner Heisenberg, and Wolfgang Pauli collaborated in their research of the nature of reality in the subatomic world. What they found was a world of paradoxes. "The more they tried to clarify the situation, the sharper the paradoxes became."[16] "The concepts of quantum theory were not easy to accept even after their mathematical formulation had been completed." The effects of the study shocked the physicists' imagination. "The subatomic units of matter are very abstract entities which have a dual aspect. Depending on how we look at them, they appear sometimes as particles, sometimes as waves; and this dual nature is also exhibited by light which can take the form of electromagnetic waves or particles."[17]

Another physicist, Max Planck, continued working on the ideas of quantum theory. He found that these particles make up "energy packets," which are fundamental aspects of nature, and called these quanta or particles "photons." "They are particles of a special kind, however, massless and always traveling with the speed of light."[18] In other words, the fundamental aspects of nature are made of light, or light waves. As a result, a basic oneness of the universe was revealed in quantum theory.

It shows that we cannot decompose the world into independently existing units. As we penetrate into matter, nature does not show us any isolated "basic building block," but rather appears as a complicated web of relations between the various parts of the whole. These relations always include the observer in an essential way. The human observer constitutes the final link in the chain of observational processes, and the properties of any atomic object can only be understood in terms of the object's interaction with the observer.[19]

To confuse matters even more, it was found that the conflicting behavior was due not to the properties of the particles themselves but from the physicist's *interaction* with these phenomena. In other words, an *interactive field in nature* was discovered. This interactive field later became known as Heisenberg's "uncertainy principle" and is the basis for understanding quantum field theory.

Quest for a Unified Theory

After the discovery of an interactive field in the micro-world, scientists began to see the macro-world from another lens as well. When the modern computer became available, complex systems also became available for investigation. "The computer enabled scientists to deal with *simultaneous* interactions among *nonlinear* processes, which led to the discovery of order in higher levels of complexity, named chaos theory. Chaos theory essentially uncovered a progressive self-organization in nature, which replaced the idea that nature was 'intrinsically unpredictable, evolutionary trajectories.'"[20]

Ervin Laszlo is considered the world's foremost proponent of systems theory and general evolution theory. He has authored 50 books and more than 300 journal articles and is known for his notion of the "Vacuum Plenum field." In *The Creative Cosmos*, Laszlo states that from these investigations, scientists began looking for a "grand unifying theory" or GUT, a new transdisciplinary cosmology. Scientists normally dealt with the observable world and did not usually go beyond that to look at the phenomena of life and mind, however, some physicists were interested in finding a "complete bootstrap theory—one that would explain progressive self-organization in nature not only in the physical world but also in the biological and the human realm"[21] as well as one that explained random change or differentiation in nature. These physicists interested in finding a unifying theory and whose views are rooted in panpsychism were Bohm, Prigogine, and Sheldrake.

"Although current GUTs describe the properties and interactions of particles, atoms and molecules, they do not show how particles, atoms, and molecules generate the various phenomena of the world we experience."[22] But GUTs did not explain the emergence of higher levels of complexity and it became a considerable problem. In other words, GUTs were not the panacea that scientists were looking for.

Laszlo emphasized that "the challenge must be faced: it is to create an empirically consistent and internally coherent theory that would rise toward the pinnacles of complexity and order in nature with better logic than either chance or speculative metaphysics can provide."[23] David Bohm was one of the scientists who faced the challenge and put forth a radical notion of reality. He proposed two levels of reality; one he termed the "implicate order" and the other, the "explicate order." In Bohm's vision of an unfolding and enfolding universe, everything is connected with everything else to form one indivisible whole. In other words, everything is interconnected through an acausal principle, just as Jung proposed in his notion of synchronicity.[24]

Bohm emphasized that both the theory of relativity and quantum mechanics indicated an unbroken wholeness of the universe; that the whole does not simply consist of parts in interaction, but that the whole organizes the parts and further, that the whole is enfolded into the parts. Imagine the universe as a net, as woven together. "The network of indivisible quanta can help us to see an underlying order which is no longer a mechanistic order, in which parts are only externally related, but an order in which everything is interconnected."[25]

I am struck by how much this recalls the way in which Jung sees synchronicity as having an organizing archetype that is underlying the manifest world. Bohm's two-level universe is a mirror image of the other, one reflecting the other. With all implicate orders, there is an explicate order that corresponds to it. Bohm's theory has been criticized as just another Duality. In addition, his model of the two-layer universe does not have a theory for evolution. In other words, "the origins of the order are not explained."[26]

Although Bohm's theory lacks an evolving component, Ilya Prigogine introduced a theory that included it. "Ilya Prigogine was among the first to realize the transdisciplinary implication of the study of evolutionary processes. A living system, he said is not like clockwork that can be explained by simple causal relations among its parts; in an organism each organ and each process is a function of the whole."[27] This idea is not unlike the notion of a hologram. Prigogine won the prestigious Nobel Prize in chemistry in 1977 for his theory in "dissipative structures" and is also known for the discovery of chaos theory and complexity theory.[28] His theory was important because it introduced "unstable bifurcation points," meaning a system can "choose" between or among more than one possible future, thereby explaining the evolution of changes among species and the nature of the universe.

The desire to find a universal theory continued. Physicists were either developing closed-system theories or open-system theories, but they could not reconcile the two opposing paradigms, which could tell a whole story regarding the nature of the universe. The basic question that Laszlo says the scientists were asking was if there exists unified structure underlying the way nature evolved or was nature just a random selection of fluctuations that were fully unpredictable? This question is directly relevant to understanding the universal field. For if there is no unified web underlying the universe, how do we interpret the experience of field-like phenomena? How is it that others or I receive identical images, or feel the somatic changes in another's body? If a unified field can be found in the natural world, would this not point to the possibility that a psychic web of energy exists as well?

Sheldrake and Morphic Resonance

Plant biologist Rupert Sheldrake developed the theory of morphic resonance following biologists' studies of the flatworm in the 1920s. His work was prompted by the question of how forms replicate themselves. How do these flatworms produce a consistent form that DNA alone cannot answer? One scientist found that there is in fact no correlation between the DNA content of species and their morphological or other complexity. For example, humans and chimpanzees are significantly different morphologically and behaviorally, yet their DNA content is extremely similar.[29]

Sheldrake further developed the idea that biological fields have a reality of their own. Though they do not carry any form of energy, they exist apart from the organism on which they act. "In consequence the theory is not limited to biology but offers a universal principle of form and order in nature."[30]

According to the hypothesis of formative causation, the morphic fields that organize our behaviour are not confined to the brain, or even to the body, but extend beyond it into the environment, like an invisible net, linking the body to the surround in which it acts.[31] Sheldrake further described the nature of morphic fields in nature by stating, "a field brings about material effects while the system is tuned in to it. But if the tuning is changed, then other fields come into play: the original field 'disappears.' It appears again when the body in relation to its environment re-enters a state similar to that in which the field was expressed before; the field once again becomes present by morphic resonance."[32] This would indicate why when someone enters a sacred place where ritual has been part of the sacred space, such as churches and monasteries; there is an overwhelming sense of a field at that site. Sheldrake called this a "stable attractor site."

Not only did Sheldrake propose the existence of a morphic field, but he also defined the differences in the field in the following quote:

> The fields that according to the present hypothesis are associated with this mental activity are therefore different from behavioral fields and can most appropriately be described as mental fields, rather than behavioral fields. These are again a kind of morphic field stabilized by morphic resonance from similar past patterns of activity. The distinction between morphogenetic, behavioral, and mental fields is of value when considering the kinds of organized activities with which these fields are associated; but it is not a hard and fast distinction. They are perhaps more like different regions of a spectrum of morphic fields.[33]

This definition describes fields as some sort of *highway* having no energy of its own, but being the thing that gives it form. This metaphorical way of thinking about a field as a "spectrum" of morphic fields aptly describes my view of how the interactive, universal field lives within some sort of form.

However, upon closer inspection states Laszlo, Sheldrake's theory runs into difficulties. Laszlo asks how can there be genuine innovation if "things are how they are because they were as they were?" In other words, how do new forms come into being? Laszlo points out that Sheldrake himself was aware of the problem and wondered in a private conversation, "if the universe is a system of habits, how do new patterns ever come into being—what is the basis of creativity? This led Sheldrake to more esoteric questions, such as 'Could creativity on Earth be a product of the imagination of a Gaian mind?'"[34]

Laszlo felt that although Sheldrake's theory represents a true physical phenomenon or field that shapes and informs organisms, it does not explicitly answer what it *is* that is responsible for the creative dynamics "whereby order emerges in space and time." This question alludes to the old "ghost in the machine" question. Coming close to defining a kind of "consciousness" in the phenomenon, Laszlo suggests that there is a subtle form—perhaps an energy field—that would code, encode, transmit, and store information and distribute it more precisely, and is also responsible for the creative nature of the universe.[35]

Laszlo answers this question by introducing a term, the "Ψ (psi)-field. He names the effect that the field produces on observable phenomena the "Ψ-effect." "Although the Ψ field does not cause event, since there are no causes for individual events, it is acausally related to the individual events since it is the underlying probability structure or order manifesting in all events."[36] I do not know if this term applied to this "something" answers the question he poses, but I feel the term he gives this seemingly unqualifiable *interactive* energy works well. Laszlo feels that his choice of this Greek symbol is not arbitrary. "First, given that the field in question is a major—though hitherto neglected—aspect of nature, it deserves a scientific name of its own. The meanings currently and traditionally associated with the symbol Ψ stand for the Schrodinger wave function as well as for *psyche*—soul, intelligence, or generally principle of life and mind—satisfy this requirement." [37] Laszlo goes on to say that the use of the Ψ (psi) for the space-time connecting field has a threefold rationale:

First: In regard to the realm of the quantum, the field completes the description of the quantum state—it further specifies the wave function of the particle.

Second: With respect to the living world, the field is a factor of self-referentiality. It "in-forms" organisms consistently with their own and their milieu's morphology and may thus be viewed as a kind of intelligence—a generalized sort of "psyche" operating in the womb of nature.

Third: In the domain of mind and consciousness, the field creates spontaneous communication between human brains as well as between the environment of the organisms possessing the brains. Though the field's effects are not limited to ESP and other esoterica, they convey the kind of information that has been traditionally subsumed in the category of "psi-phenomena."[38]

Laszlo described the brain as having "band-width" psi-field receptivity, and that it enlarges in altered states of consciousness. After describing many studies using EEG brain patterns, he concludes that the psi-field can explain:

- Telepathic communication between individuals
- Past life recollections
- Natural healing
- Simultaneous insights among individuals as well as between cultures.[39]

Significantly, Laszlo links his ideas of the psi-field to Jung's concept of the collective unconscious and the reality of archetypes. He quotes the following from Jung:

It could be that the psyche is an unextended intensity, not a body moving in time. One could assume that the psyche arises gradually from the smallest extension to an infinite intensity and thus robs bodies of their reality when the psychic intensity transcends the speed of light. Our brain might be the place of transformation, where the relatively infinite tensions or intensities of the psyche are tuned down to perceptible *frequencies* [emphasis added] and extensions.[40]

Jung saw modern physics as analogies for psychic processes. At the same time he could see that, in dealing with subatomic particles, the physicists were dealing with entities that could not directly be represented, just as ultimately the archetypes could not be represented.[41]

This leads back "beyond" the archetype to a place in which instinct and archetype are united as opposites in the primary patterns of human behavior. It leads back to what Jung called the *psychoid factor*.[42] Jung believed that psychoid factor was a process that touched fundamental unconscious aspects of the psyche. He stated that these unconscious aspects occurring at the psychoid level might appear in hypnosis, dreams, in trance, or in other variations of altered states of consciousness, or it may erupt in somatic ways causing skin rashes, heart conditions, and ulcers to name a few, all of which may automatically disappear when the psychic source is resolved. Reaching the psychoid layers of the psyche depends on another factor or condition, which Jung termed *Abaissement du niveau mental* referring to a partial lowering of the mental level. This lowering of consciousness would be like a defocusing, a softening of the mental focus. This dropping down, so to speak, is perhaps what Pribram referred to as responding selectively to a bandwidth of frequencies, not unlike tuning into a particular radio wave frequency.

This is how Jung defines this "lower down" place in the psyche:

The deeper "layers" of the psyche lose their individual uniqueness as they retreat farther and farther into darkness. "Lower down." That is to say as they approach the autonomous functional systems, they become increasingly collective until they are universalized and extinguished in the body's materiality, i.e., in chemical substances. The body's carbon is merely carbon. Hence, at the bottom, the psyche is simple "world."[43]

That is to say that at some point there is no differentiation between self and world, and that this level of the psyche can manifest either psychically or somatically.

Holograms versus the Hierarchy

In addition to the aforementioned paradigms outlined earlier by de Quincey, there are two other paradigms in the paradigm "arguments." The argument between these seemingly contradictive notions are taken up quite often in philosophical, religious, and scientific literature. The argument goes back to the question, once again, of whether the universe moves in an organized autonomous progressive way, like Jung's individuation process, or whether the world is organized in a more holographic, multidimensional, and circular way. More to the point is the question—are psi-fields fine webs or highways leading somewhere, like in Sheldrake's morphic fields, or do they exist in a vacuum—a vast space—like the ocean in which the creatures live in and with, as envisioned by the holonomic constructs?

The hologram has been widely used in popular literature to describe and perhaps define the nature of the universe. Michael Talbot, for example in the *Holographic Universe*, believes that this remarkable new theory of reality in the latest frontiers in physics is a panacea explaining everything unanswerable from paranormal abilities of the mind, including synchronicity, to unsolved riddles of brain and body.

I propose that we look for a moment at this idea as a possibility of integrating these notions of consciousness and the nature of the universe. Talbot introduces the theoretical stance that not only is the universe a hologram, but the brain is also. He then goes into detail describing why—from this model—paranormal realities and mystical experiences can co-exist in our physical universe and make perfect sense within the holographic model. He states that this model could shed light on an increasing number of previously inexplicable phenomena. Here are some of Talbot's examples from his book:

> In 1980 University of Connecticut psychologist Dr. Kenneth Ring proposed that near-death experiences could be explained by the holographic model . . . he believes that such experiences are nothing more than the shifting of a person's consciousness from one level of the hologram of reality to another.
> In 1985 Dr. Stanislav Grof, chief of psychiatric research at the Maryland Psychiatric Research Center, published a book in which he concluded that existing neurophysiological models of the brain are inadequate and only a holographic model can explain such things as archetypal experiences, encounters with the collective unconscious, and other unusual phenomena experienced during altered states of consciousness.

> At the 1987 annual meeting of the Association for the Study of Dreams held in Washington, DC, physicist Fred Alan Wolf delivered a talk in which he asserted that the holographic model explains lucid dreams. Wolf believes such dreams are actually visits to parallel realities, and the holographic model will ultimately allow us to develop a "physics of consciousness," which will enable us to begin to explore more fully these other-dimensional levels of existence.

> In his 1987 book *Synchronicity: the Bridge Between Matter and Mind,* Dr. F. David Peat, a physicist at Queen's University in Canada, asserted that synchronicities can be explained by the holographic model . . . They reveal that our thought processes are much more intimately connected to the physical world than has been hitherto suspected.[44]

Talbot relays the history of the holographic theory citing the main architects who are two of the world's most eminent thinkers: David Bohm, one of the world's most respected quantum physicists whom I introduced earlier, and Karl Pribram, a neurophysiologist at Stanford University. They hypothesize that the entire physical universe is composed of a web of subatomic particles that make up "the very fabric of reality itself," which possesses what appears to be an undeniable "holographic" property.[45] "As for Pribram, by the 1970s, enough evidence had accumulated to convince him his theory was correct. In addition, he had taken his ideas into the laboratory and discovered that single neurons in the motor cortex of the brain respond selectively to limited bandwidth of frequencies."[46]

The question that Pribram began to formulate was that if the picture of reality in our brain is not a picture at all but a hologram, what is it a hologram of?

The dilemma posed by this question is analogous to taking a Polaroid picture of a group of people sitting around a table and, after the picture develops, finding that instead of people, there are only blurry clouds of interference patterns positioned around the table. In both cases one could rightfully ask, which is the true reality, the seemingly objective world experienced by the observer–photographer or the blur of interference patterns recorded by the camera–brain? Pribram realized that if the holographic brain model was taken to its logical conclusions, it opened the door on the possibility that objective reality—the world of coffee cups, mountain vistas, elm trees, and table lamps—might not even exist, or at least not exist in the way we believe it exists. Was it possible, he wondered, that what the mystics had been saying for centuries was true, reality was *Maya,* an illusion, and what was out there was really a vast, resonating symphony of wave forms, a "frequency domain" that was transformed into the world as we know it only *after* it entered our senses?[47]

With this in mind, let's turn our attention back to Bohm's holographic image. He believes that underlying the holographic image is a deeper order of existence that gives way to a vast and more primary level of reality that gives birth to all the objects and appearances of our physical world in much the same way that a piece of holographic film gives birth to a hologram.[48] Bohm, you will recall, is the physicist who developed the concept of two levels of reality. He called the deeper level of reality the *implicate* order (which means enfolded order), and refers to our own level of existence as the *explicate,* or unfolded order. He uses these terms because he sees the manifestation of all forms in the universe as the result of countless enfoldings and unfolding between these two orders, therefore preferring to think of the universe as a "holomovement."[49]

In an interview with Ken Wilber, a transpersonal philosopher, David Bohm defined his notion of the holographic model: "The holographic model of consciousness is based on the notion that information from which the consciousness works is not stored in particular places but rather is stored all over the brain or over large areas of the brain, and each time the information is used, a selection is made by gathering it together from all over as happens with the hologram outside the brain."[50] However, Bohm did not want to push the analogy too far, recognizing that the hologram produces only a static record whereas reality is dynamic—characterized by the constant unfoldment and enfoldment of the implicate/explicate order.[51]

Going back to his question of the Polaroid picture, "a piece of holographic film and the image it generates is an example of an implicate and explicate order. The film is an implicate order because the image is encoded in its interference patterns in a hidden totality enfolded throughout the whole. The hologram projected from the film is an explicate order because it represents the unfolded and perceptible version of the image."[52]

Pribram has suggested that all perception of the outside world is dependent on a "frequency domain," which, like the ripples in the pond, needs to be decoded. The frequency domain can be regarded as an intermediate zone between the object and the image.[53] This intermediate zone is not unlike Ibn'Arabi's imaginal realm and I believe Pribram is giving us a clue as to how the psi-field or universal field *interacts* in the universal energy fields.

Reflecting on the idea of frequencies, radio waves and the visible spectrum of light have very different properties; for example, one can go through walls and the other cannot. Yet they are different levels of an underlying electromagnetic spectrum.[54] Woodhouse eloquently states:

> Of all the flowing energies in the universe, consciousness is the most dominant, the one from which all the others proceed and into which they all merge. The ancient texts are fond of the phrase, "from consciousness down to the solid Earth," for all this is a single matrix, a tantra, of energy, and within it are myriads of matrices, woven and interwoven. The human being is one such matrix of energies—ebbing, flowing, dancing at frequencies ranging from those of solid bones all the way to the subtlest wave of consciousness.[55]

This dynamic and delightful description of the human being as "a dancing matrix of flowing energies" gives us a wonderful sense of the universal fields in and around us.

Again, I am struck by the use of the word frequencies in the many descriptions of the spectrum of consciousness.

I have so far explored the holonomic or holographic model of reality, which seems to present a plausible view of reality. However, Wilber cautions us regarding this view. In a reprint of an interview with the journal *ReVision*, Wilber states why the hologram model is problematic. He says that the problem with the popular holographic theories, as well as the general "new physics and Eastern mysticism stuff" is that these theories collapse the hierarchy. They go from saying, "All shadows are ultimately illusory" to saying, "All shadows are equally illusory." That is, the theories latch on to such phrases as "All things are One:" or "Separate entities don't exist" or "Isolated things are merely shadows" and then overlook the distinctions between the shadows themselves. They (the holographic theories) collapse the shadows and they collapse the hierarchy.[56]

Wilber believes that this is the error of pantheistic models, that they collapse the hierarchy into one big pot of soup. For example, he states that biology cannot be explained only in terms of physics, psychology cannot be explained only in terms of biology, and so on. Each senior stage includes its junior stages as components but also transcends them by adding its own defining attributes.[57]

Another example Wilber gives is of the three-dimensional cube that contains two-dimensional squares, but not vice versa. Wilber is a proponent of the Great Chain of Being, or sometimes called the Perennial Philosophy. This idea of "hierarchical interpenetration" stipulates that higher levels enfold and permeate lower levels and are thus more inclusive, with each level possessing characteristics that others do not, and hence are relatively distinct. "Yet all are permeated by the highest level, the source of all things."[58]

Wilber further explains the difference between a hierarchy, which he sometimes refers to as a "holo-archy" and holography. "Each stage-level of the hierarchy is, as Huston Smith pointed out, a more or less unified totality that can stand on its own, so to speak. Likewise, all of the elements of each level are said to be mutually interdependent and interrelated. Each level of hierarchy, in other words, is a type of holography—they interact, but not in a mutual or absolutely equivalent fashion, and for the simple reason that they aren't equivalent."[59]

So, if each level of the hierarchy in the Great Chain of Being contains a type of holographic structure, we could say that this is a form that holds the interpenetrating fields that resemble Sheldrake's morphic fields. This seems to be why there is more than one web in the universal field. They in fact exist at many levels: the biological, the psychological, and probably in the spiritual, or transpersonal, realms to which the yogis allude.

Wilber admits that the human brain may store information holographically, yet he makes an important point not to collapse everything to one thing. He states that in the process of storing information the brain translates it from a dynamic or moving state into a "timeless" or stored condition. But this timeless or frozen condition has little to do with a metaphysical or mystical eternity. Wilber believes an eternity that would be dependent for its existence on a temporal structure, a tape or brain, would be a strange eternity.

In other words, the brain reads frequencies, but even in the frequency realm there is some sort of structure. And the structure cannot be confused with that which is radically without structure, or perfectly dimensionless, transcendent and infinite.[60] I cannot definitely say whether the universal field, or psi-fields, move into the metaphysical realms, but will say that since archetypes are the patterns of the universe and are universal patterns, I would think that a universal field is no less "alive" there as well. However, once someone evolves to the highest state of being, as I understand it, there may only be stillness, which is perhaps the ultimate threshold experience.

It is difficult to see outside our own habitual and entrenched views of the world because we are so influenced by the materialist paradigm; as Koestler and others have pointed out that the Cartesian tradition to identify "mind" with "conscious thinking" is deeply engrained in our habits of thought, and we constantly forget the obvious, trivial fact that consciousness is not an all-or-nothing affair but a matter of degrees. "There is a continuous scale of gradations which extends from the unconsciousness that results from being hit on the head, through the restricted forms of consciousness in dreamless sleep."[61]

The definition of consciousness that Woodhouse gives fits with my own understanding of the nature of consciousness: "consciousness is the inner subjective aspect of energy and that energy, whether in physical forms or in forms not currently recognized by physics, is the outward objective aspect of consciousness…Consciousness and energy are complementary aspects of each other"[62] just as psyche and matter are complementary aspects of one another and are different only by degrees in a spectrum or continuum.

It seems to me that the universal mind is a device that ascertains levels of energy, but it is not the energy, just as consciousness is not the mind, but rather, is like the radio receiver for it. But unlike the radio analogy, once the "radio" picks up the frequency, the archetypal signatures within the frequency then surreptitiously reorganize the soma/psyche. I will speak more to this idea in Chapter Seven when looking at the subtle body as a threshold place.

Woodhouse continues by elucidating the properties that consciousness and energy share by stating, "both energy and consciousness satisfy the same text-book definition as the 'power to produce change.' Finally, both are most adequately understood as underlying fields which may express themselves in particulate form as thoughts, sensations, etc., in the case of consciousness, or as electrons and photons in the case of quantum theory."[63]

Author and Jungian analyst, Michael Conforti and physicist, David Peat were discussing these very questions in a personal conversation about how the fields interact and how the archetypal fields may influence them. Conforti thought that Peat made an important contribution to this issue:

> Not only is there some sort of non-local correlation but also something almost tangible that is localized... Maybe there are physical fields that become entrained into the archetypal field. I'm not sure this isn't just two different manifestations of the one phenomenon. Maybe the local fields are different and actually use some sort of biological energy or energy associated with physical locations. But their form is influenced by the archetypal, non-local field."[64]

This last statement leads me to question how shamen move about in the different realms. The idea that physical fields become entrained provides a clue as to how they are able to travel to different "worlds" or realms. The metaphor of the tree or ladder, the reader will recall, is often used as the "highway" or method of travel. Could shamen be projecting their subtle body or accessing an interactive field in which they travel with the their consciousness?

Perhaps there are local fields entrained by morphic resonance; in other words, by using them over and over until they become imbued as a place—a place of power—or a way to move about in the realms of nature and psyche. Places of power are found all over the world. These sacred sites have been revered for centuries and have been known to have some sort of "*mana.*" "Scientific studies conducted at many of these sites reveal the presence of higher than normal electromagnetic frequencies. If these findings and inferences being drawn are correct, they may provide a scientific explanation for why people are effected [sic] by place, and how place and land expresses certain archetypal constants."[65]

Louise von Franz, a close colleague of Jung, often spoke of a psychic energy, which she saw as the force driving the unfolding of events. Von Franz often referred to "excited points" in the archetypal fields, which corresponded to synchronistic events. Instead of excited points, many authors use the radio analogy that compares the workings of radio stations in which each station tends to represent a certain genre of music—say one station plays jazz while the other plays rock or classical music. The concept of the "eternal now," referred to by many authors, is the idea that past, present, and future may actually exist simultaneously but in different vibrational time frames. "By shifting the frequency focus of one's consciousness, one may be able to tune into specific time frames outside of the present. In actuality, by shifting one's frequency focus, one may be shifting his/her consciousness from the viewing perspective of the physical up to the astral, mental casual, and higher energetic levels which are all a part of our total energetic expression."[66]

It is impossible to not refer to the numinous when you begin to experience these "archetypal frequencies" as transformative events. "One senses from the above that we are on the verge of rediscovering what the mystics, alchemists, and poets have known for centuries—namely the existence of an *unus mundis*."[67] *one world or cosmos.*

Recent studies suggest that patients who have received organ transplants actually exhibit behaviors and tendencies of the unknown organ donor. Gail Schwarz and Linda Russek, in their book *The Living Energy Universe*, from the perspective of the field theory, suggest that the transplanted bodily part remains connected to the donor's field, carrying with it, as does a hologram, a composite of the individual's life and tendencies.[68] The authors devote a whole section to amazing stories of heart recipients. In these stories heart transplant recipients tell uncanny stories of how their lives changed. After receiving the transplant, for example, they often began liking certain foods, or doing things they had never done before. Upon investigation, it was found that these were the very foods, habits, and behaviors the donor had while alive. The personal story of one woman's experience with this can be read in the book *The Heart's Code* by Paul Pearsall. This obviously implies that some sort of consciousness of the donor is entrained or merges—interacts—with the recipient of the organ. Do heart recipients react to some sort of archetypal entrainment? Most certainly they are experiencing Sheldrake's morphogenetic fields.

I realize that this chapter has been only a compendium of an in-depth subject that has filled volumes of research. I also know that I could not possibly do justice to the notion of a universal field without some kind of review of the scientific body of work within the quantum "fields." As Woodhouse so aptly states:

> "We are consciousness looking for itself, trying to give itself an identity by what it can objectify. We are on the inside looking out, suffering from the illusion of identifying with what we find, but suspecting there may be something more. So we take up the search again by seeming to look for ourselves on the inside of things but from an outside perspective. Our search is based upon the reciprocal perspective of what makes it possible in the first place. As long as we live in the duality of inside and outside, we are doomed to fail. However, our struggle in time will bring us closer to the realization that we are both sides, straddling, as it were, a duality that as only relative, never absolute!"[69]

"Many authors have used the holographic analogy to say that it exemplifies what the mystics have always known about consciousness and the reality of the world. They say that the entire world is *maya*, or illusion. Heisenberg's uncertainty principle has been used to advance the argument that "nothing is absolute" as it replicates the nature of the universe according to quantum theorists. All these debates, speculations, and worldviews lead to the question of the autonomy of images within the universal field. It asks us to question the nature of the universal field as either a predetermined form, or a constellated, perhaps even evoked condition in nature or psyche or both.

Through the Looking Glass: The Problem with Memory

Authors often write about mind and consciousness interchangeably. I would like to make a distinction between the two. I think of mind as being different from consciousness in that mind belongs to man, and consciousness may be a broader concept; it "goes all the way down" following the panpsychic view. This allows that consciousness may be present in all sentient beings, but not only in mind. For me, mind is connected to the brain of humans. My mind is the personal conscious, the ego, and the personal unconscious, "all that I am not aware of." "Sacred Mind," a term coined by author, Christopher Bache, or universal mind includes all sentient beings, or what Jung called the psyche (collective unconscious).

I like the notion that de Quincy puts forth in that consciousness is not an object, but rather a process.[70] He states that this move from object to process requires a shift in our thinking. Throughout this book I refer to a state of consciousness, which points to a thing rather than a process, but I actually think it is both. Metaphorically, it seems that consciousness is like air: air can inhabit a balloon, so to speak, and it can move dynamically as wind. I wonder if consciousness can also inhabit a field? Can it travel within an energetic form, or embed itself in form with information ready to be accessed by those who understand how to reveal it? I make the conjecture that it can.

This brings us to the question of memory and what it actually is. Does memory only have to do with the function of our brain, or can it reside in things, such a stones, as some people believe? When memory and information are stored, are they stored in the same manner, and where exactly is it stored? Both research scientists and philosophers have wrestled with these as well as other questions.

On the other side of perennial philosophy is Pribram's theory in which he states that memory is nonlocal and resides in some sort of hologram to be retrieved by various methods. Some authors have proposed that memory is retrievable from a magnetic field that exists around the brain (or around plants, rocks, trees?). I believe this field actually exists around the whole body. Similar to the Akashic Record that is referred to in metaphysical sources, memory is accessible through various means and is not time-bound. We have seen that because of the holographic nature of the psyche, the psyche can holographically move about to any "time, place, or event."

My own experience of memory and consciousness leads me to feel more aligned with this notion that the psyche is more of a hologram, rather than to locate images *in* the brain, or coming from the brain as many materialists do. You can find this view in many of the left–right brain studies. This materialistic approach is for me as fruitless as trying to locate people in the television set. Thus memory would be seen as having a linear time construct. Memory is seen as a series of this–then–thats. However, the linear time construct does not allow for the psyche's ability to move beyond time, or outside of "space-time." Like a strand of pearls, linear memory is useful in our lives; it gives our history meaning and structure to the moments that have sculpted how we see ourselves. We need our memories, but they are not who we are at the substrate of our being. We are so much more than those moments that seem to shape our lives.

For me, retrieving memory is a different use of the mind than when retrieving lived moments or experiences via altered states. Memory is a left-brain activity, where I engage my thinking function. Remembering is something you do. There seems to be another kind of memory that does not have anything to do with the mind's capacity to remember. It has more to do with the unconscious memory of the body, which seems to store memory encoded in cellular form, and includes an emotional aspect that may be accessed through non-ordinary states of consciousness. I have the sense that the emotional body gets activated when we enter a somatic field, or the subtle field around the body (I will delve more extensively into this idea in Chapter Six). Below is an example from my own life of how a linear memory and a feeling state can be simultaneously stored in two different areas of the soma/psyche.

As long as I could "remember," I had the experience of tears welling up every time an ambulance drove by with its sirens roaring. I could never understand why this always happened, and no matter how hard I tried, I could not stop the tears from coming. One day, an ambulance was coming toward me with its light and sirens on full blast. I pulled over, and began asking myself what this tearfulness could be about? Because I was in a light trance state from driving, I immediately went into a spontaneous "flashback."

79

I was ten years old and holding on to my mother's right hand. My arm was extended up to hold her hand as I stood next to her at the front door. I watched as my father was being taken away in an ambulance. He had just had a heart attack while I was rubbing his back. He began moaning and rolling back and forth. I screamed for my mother to come and she immediately called for help.

The helplessness and terror I felt that day had been locked away in my somatic field. I had no "memory" of it; I did not remember it. As I relived this event in a timeless moment on the side of a busy highway, I re-experienced the terror once again and the fear that I had somehow killed my father. The interesting thing is that in remembering my childhood I had a very clear "memory" of my father's heart attack that had nearly killed him. I easily "remembered" this aspect of the event and could tell you how old I was when that happened. What I had dissociated from was the emotional affect of that memory. Since retrieving that emotional state that I had unconsciously buried, strangely enough I have never teared up again at the sound of an ambulance. It was as if the linking of the memory with the emotional trauma freed my body from its cellular, traumatic memory. In this case, I am not sure that "cellular" memory is where this memory was stored. Could it have been stored in some holographic field that was accessed when I asked for information? No matter where it was stored, I feel this experience adequately describes how linear memory is something different than spontaneous recall, which includes imagery and affect.

Researchers in the "repressed memory" argument have hotly debated whether memory from recall is contaminated by emotional affect, and therefore unreliable, or even whether there is such a thing a repressed memory. From my personal experience, and that of my clients, memories can easily be repressed because the horror from trauma is usually what creates the amnesia. Sometimes the only way to access these kinds of stored memories is only through a shift in consciousness or through imaginal states. These are other kinds of portals into realms that seem to contain an energetic field that when accessed produce dramatic changes in the psyche as well as in the body. Whether the memories are reliable may be debatable, however this is not really what is relevant when it involves the need to heal from emotional trauma. What is important is that psyche is able to access imagery for this purpose.

Staying within the metaphor of left brain/right brain thinking, on the other side of linear memory, is right-brain thinking—if it could be called that at all—that is accessed through a lowering of consciousness, an *abaissement du niveau mental*. The right brain is associated with non-ordinary states of consciousness, creativity, holism, images and oracular experiences, to name a few, and may be the gateways through which we experience liminal time and synchronicity. These threshold experiences do not live in the realm of memory although this may be where we store them once they have become lived experience, for later recall. The experience of an emotional affect, spontaneous image, or an oracular knowing comes from a lowering of the mental activity, which may be like a right-brain experience that occurs in non-ordinary states of consciousness and is anchored in a somatic response.

Jung believed we must seriously entertain the idea that these kinds of experiences are autonomous, having free agency. He said that imagery, spontaneous images, oracular experiences, and synchronicity are examples of experience that have a "mind" of their own, do what they want to do, and may not be the result of our personal psyche's volition. If this is so, then we must ask, how is it that they interact with us, not to mention *why*? I can't presume to know why, but I believe it is through the psi-fields in the universal web that these phenomena interact with us. Perhaps, then, Sheldrake was correct to say that the fields have no energy by themselves, but are more like the conduits of the energy that manifests as imagery in the field. Jung struggled with this question and seemed to continually solve the dualistic "this or that" problem. Jung seemed to always go back to the psychoid for his answer, which is to say that at some point it is no longer possible to determine what is me and not me. Unlike memories, spontaneous or autonomous images may be either part of my psyche, part of our psyche, or come into the field from the collective psyche, and therefore can be autonomous at many levels.

Chapter Four

Unchained Memories

*The universe is a dance of energies which vibrate at
many frequencies. They ebb and flow, merge and part,
form ripples, tides, currents, eddies, and whirlpools.
They become units of all sizes, from atoms to stars,
individual souls to cosmic beings . . . As rays, streaks,
streams, rivers, oceans of light, they flow into each
other and separate again, changing frequencies—and
changing frequencies, they become suns, galaxies,
spaces, airs, winds, fires, liquids, solids. They become
the bodies of human beings into which the energy
called consciousness comes and is embodied.*

-Swami Rama

Psyche's Stories

The psyche loves to tell stories. It tells them every night in
dreamtime. It comes through fairytales and in our myths to tell a
story. Perhaps it's the story that wants to be told, and finds its own
portals through which to be heard. It comes through dreams, art,
poetry, dance, and in soul journeys, which are framed in past-life
vignettes. It is as if the story, when it finally gets to tell its tale,
surrenders its hold on us. Our job is to understand the language of the
psyche. Psyche is a Greek word meaning "Soul." We might as easily

call past-life expressions *soul stories*. I refer to this kind of work in therapy as "Holographic Journeying." Holographic journeying is an interactive imagery framed in the notion of past lives, yet is a more holistic construct modeled after the holographic notion of the eternal now (See the last chapter for a more in-depth look at this idea). It is a regression into another time period in now-time, played out in the imagery of virtual lives. It is also a portal into a threshold of non-linear time, waiting to be accessed, replayed and reviewed for our awakening of the Self.

What if past life expressions were like waking dreams—life dreams—enveloped in templates familiar to mankind? Are these templates, enveloped in life dreams, life-like replays that are magnificently situated in an energetic field or life issue? What else could so explicitly underline and shift our stories releasing us from the magnetic pull that draws us over and over to the same wavelength or life pattern until we find a way through these waking dreams framed in past-life vignettes?

Emotional and mental disorders are encoded organically or cellularly, and are not always easily available from the "memory banks." We saw this in my example from childhood and the effect the ambulance sirens had on me in the last chapter. Until I had that spontaneous recall, the sound of the ambulance sirens was not consciously linked to the emotional impact my father's heart attack had on me. It is only through an altered state of consciousness that we are able to retrieve "state-bound information."

Hypnotherapy often refers to ego states that are state bound, which means that some part of the psyche has been split off and is only available through some sort of retrieval method. Shamanic journeying in soul retrieval work is based on this idea, as if these state bound affective patterns live in an archetypal field, waiting for the correct access code to release them. These state-bound matrixes of energy and trauma—which Jung termed complexes— are often triggered and re-experienced as uncontrollable bodily experiences, unrelated emotional affects, or compulsions that are unlinked to an actual event. In regression work, all of these somatic and affective states are portals through and to the release of the trauma that lies at the root of these experiences living in an unconscious matrix. Jung said that embedded in every complex is an archetype, an archetypal field that once made conscious, releases its hold on us.

Consider a person who has a life pattern or theme that prevents him from moving forward into his soul's potential. In Holographic Journey work, or translife regressions, a person enters an altered state, which then allows the psyche to create the perfect holographic experience that can set this person free from his/her pattern. As we saw in Chapter Three, in a holographic paradigm, time and space are arbitrary constructs of the psyche. This concept allows the psyche to move through the collective unconscious, or the universal web, holographically "landing" in the perfect drama or soul story. Some experts feel that we have a genetic memory encoded in our DNA that is imprinted in our cells and which is why we may feel drawn to or repelled by certain places, things, or idiosyncrasies. Many belief systems and traditions hold that we bring themes from many lifetimes forward through karmic patterns for the souls' evolution. Although this belief remains in a linear time construct, it nevertheless coincides with many religious traditions from cultures all over the world.

Seeing our life process as a linear series of incarnations might be only partly true within the illusion of time. There may be a reference point from which reincarnation might more accurately be described as "multiple incarnations being lived simultaneously."[1]

In regression therapy, the belief a person holds does not matter. It's sole—soul—purpose is therapeutic. You may enter into these panoramic enlivened fields as if they were real. However, to the psyche they are real—they are not just "like" lived experiences, they *are* lived experiences. And like numinous experiences, or synchronistic events, they change us and are rarely forgotten experiences that tend to become guiding moments in our lives.

All of my life I have questioned the meaning of life itself. My search led me to study the "occult" at a very young age. In those days you could find me in a back corner of some library looking for metaphysical books. Bookstores had very small sections of metaphysical books usually listed in the occult section, if they had one at all. Along with my incessant curiosity, I also had a well-intended inner critic–analyst. This part questioned everything and, for me, it wasn't until I had the experience of something that I could decide for myself about it. Thinking that there was no other way to determine if this notion of reincarnation had any substance, I overrode my fear and found a hypnotherapist to decide for myself if this could possibly be "true." I had originally thought that perhaps a hypnotherapist was leading the person under hypnosis by asking specific questions. I decided to see for myself. With a tape recorder in hand, I hired a hypnotherapist to take me into past lives. Although he had never done this kind of work, he agreed to try it.

After an induction, I found myself standing outside a large southern mansion with several white columns supporting the front portico. I saw many people standing in the front yard, eating and talking. The women were dressed in long, bustled dresses, with parasols, and the men were also formally dressed. The hypnotherapist asked me what I was doing.

"I am standing here waiting for my brother." As I answered this question I could see I was a little distance from the party on what felt like a plantation.

"How old are you?"

"I am twelve," I reply, in a child-like voice.

"Where is your brother?" the therapist asks.

"He's swimmin' in the crick" I reply in a southern accent.

"How come you're not swimming?"

"Little girls don't swim!" I state emphatically.

Even as I heard myself say this, I was surprised. I had swam all of my life and in fact had been on a swim team as a child. Moving forward in that life, I found that I was to be married to a landowner who lived on a farm nearby. The marriage was arranged to keep the land in both families' names. I was quite a bit younger than this man who was named Tom Brundage. My name was Amy Bainbridge and it was just before the Civil War broke out. I said that I lived in Georgetown, Georgia. When asked what kinds of crops were grown on the land, I said "wheat fields." What was significant for me was that I experienced the death of a child during childbirth in that life. I could never have any other children in that life as I was too small to carry them and my husband, who wanted a son to inherit the family name and lands, became estranged from me. I lived and died a lonely life at the age of 50 from typhoid fever.

The reason this was significant was because in my present life I was terrified of childbirth. I thought perhaps I might have had many children in other lives, and this was the reason I was so terrified. My first labor was traumatic; it was long, and painful. My body fought it all the way, and I was bruised from the inside out after the birth of my first child. I never thought I wanted to go through another delivery. Several years after this regression, I did get pregnant, and delivered a healthy boy. That time I was fully prepared. The birth was easy and I had no terror whatsoever. Could my terror have been released from the regression work? I was not sure at that time.

The most amazing part of the story though is this: During a part of the regression, the therapist asked where my husband was. I said he had gone to town for supplies. He asked how far away the town was, and I replied, "About a day's ride." When I got home, I looked up Georgetown, Georgia in my atlas. I have never been to Georgia, and did not actually know if there was a Georgetown in Georgia at the time of the regression, at least not consciously. But there it was, and eerily, on one side of Georgetown was a town named Brundage, and on another side, a town named Bainbridge. I couldn't believe my eyes! Not only that, but in those days those two towns would have been about a day's ride by horse and buggy.

I do not know why I said "wheat fields" in the session. In my history lessons, I had only heard about cotton or tobacco crops being grown in the south. To this day I do not know if wheat was grown in the south, but hope to find out one of these days on a visit to the state of Georgia. Another synchronicity is that I always had to stop and gaze at this one particular old home in the bay area near where I lived at that time. It was a white house with white columns lining the covered front porch. I was very drawn to this house, but never knew why. I only knew that I always stopped and looked at it. It turned out to be a house just like the one I lived in on the plantation, only a much smaller version!

Needless to say, I felt that the life I reviewed had a virtual reality to it. It was as if I was that person named Amy, and I relived her fear, loneliness and the relief at the time of her death. I was convinced by that time that past lives were a reality. Now with the study of quantum physics, and the holographic notion of the universe, I am not sure. The nonlocal, nonlinear objective psyche in its multiplicity may have the capacity to review and relive any life in the archives we call history. Perhaps, like an actor in the play of life, the psyche puts on any costume it needs, and reanimates a drama for its own growth.

Holographic Soul Journeys

Holographic journeying allows the psyche to experience or re-experience key themes that come alive through imagery in a non-ordinary state of consciousness. Thus regression work becomes an imaginal production that allows one to travel through the portals of time to access the perfectly framed life related to a problem, to relive it through imagery to unlock the archetypal pattern that has a hold on a person. More importantly, I feel this work opens patterns held in the collective level—or the world psyche—and when a person endeavors upon this work, some say it actually lifts the vibrational rate and the healing for others on the planet. In other words, not only do we transform ourselves, our work affects others when we look at the cosmic hologram of reality, in that every part affects the whole. Each person working toward consciousness is in effect reverberating out to all others. While this is a huge concept to digest, it seems that it is supported by the quantum theories in Chapter Three, especially when considering the notion of entrainment, morphic resonance, and attractor templates.

I have conducted many holographic regressions—soul journeys—in my work as a therapist. People often come in with an issue that seems long-standing, which has not been resolved through "traditional" kinds of therapies. As a result of these re-animated experiences, I have found that people are often released from the pattern or theme in their current life. By entering these imaginal re-constellations framed in the linear model of time, major changes occur as a result.

Here is a story of a woman I'll call Cheryl who came in questioning why she has held herself back in life. She felt blocked in her self-expression and from seeing herself working in more creative ways.

The story opens with finding herself in a tomb. From her transcript, she begins,

"It is dusty, damp, with yellow/reddish stone. It's dark. I am dark skinned. I am looking up from the feet of a big-breasted, beautiful girl. She is in a pinkish-white cotton dress, brown hair, looking off toward the jungle. I am ankle-height to her, standing in a stairway which goes down to a square entrance underground. I love her. She is clean, I have dirty, brown peasant feet and short, ragged grayish pants that are dirty. I am a young man, maybe thirteen. I am digging and building a chamber for her, like I am part of a crew, though I can't see anyone else. She is very important. I am struck by her beauty; I adore her. I am constructing this for her, but someone else ordered it. It's a tomb, in a tropical area like Palenque or Peru. She's lighter skinned than I am. I am beneath her in all ways!"

Moving forward in time:

"They kill her and put her in the tomb. Sacrifice. It's what they do. I am not sure if I was buried alive with her too. I don't care, I want nothing more to do with them. It was wrong! I am angry."

"I'm in the dark. Inside of me and outside. In the tomb. I never want to go back up there. She's under a stone slab. I am thirsty, thin, weak. I am draped across her stone. I feel sad, and scared."

I ask her what connections she is making to this life. "I think it is not okay to be beautiful. Rules; it is not my place to change things or love her. I made the decision that people are without compassion and fairness. Don't argue with them or struggle, just go away. Don't speak out to change things! I turn away, shut up, shut down, die. In this life I didn't have a right to speak either. We don't have a right as a child."

In another life with a similar pattern, Cheryl experiences herself in a Chinese or Japanese life. She continues:

"I see a fancy outfit. She is powerful, noisy, has a yellow and red streamer and a mask of paint on her face. She could be a Japanese dancer. She's forceful—dominant" (pause). "I can't find me."

After a minute: "I have on black cloth slippers and white cloth binding on them. I am a geisha girl. I have big black hair. I am bowing. And bowing. To the flashy person, and others. I am not performing, but serving. Acting very humble. I am acting completely subservient, but that's not how I feel. There is a lot of clanging and noise. Maybe that other one is performing, or is a ruler performing a ruler role. I feel small. Quiet. A role. My role is so narrow."

"These rules! There are so many. Everything is bound by rules. Who gets to dance sing, make noise. Everything's prescribed. There is nothing I can do outside of the rules."

"Next I am sitting with three men and at least one other geisha, the more famous and powerful one. I want to sing. A man I am drawn to does ask me to sing. I begin singing. As a woman, I cannot say no to him, because he is the patron. The famous geisha makes fun of me while I am singing. I feel very humiliated. They all laugh with her. Later she scratches my face and pulls my hair because he asked me, not her. She tells me that she is the only one who gets to sing, she is the popular one. I crumble, get away and sob on a mat. There is no hope. I become dispirited and give up. I am silent and the man loses interest in me. She won't tolerate rivals and has to be the prima donna. She has to be the only one, I hate her. Turning my back on all of them, I jump into the river, which is shallow. I see my dress tumbling down the river as I leave my body in its death."

I asked Cheryl what connections she made from that life to this one. She said her mother would not tolerate competition in this lifetime, was verbally vicious and told her not to sing in church. She grew up terrified of her mother's rage and jealousy. "She was the queen." She said she thought that the woman in her past life who humiliated her in public and her mother were the same soul. She said that she always shrank back in the face of her mother's wrath and her father's "rules." Cheryl said that she learned if you break the rules you die, or if you step outside your place they will kill you.

"There is only place for one star."

From examining these lives in a virtual reality, Cheryl saw that she had several beliefs that kept her from expressing herself more fully in this life. She saw how and why she held herself back. She said she saw her mindset as:

"I have to follow the rules, no questions asked. Rules are rigid, prescribed. I didn't deserve to love, express, sing, speak. Others were more important. I wasn't."

"I didn't realize I had these beliefs and choices to do things differently."

Cheryl told me that there had been many times in her life that she had wanted to commit suicide. Although she never acted on them, the feelings were intense. Since our session, Cheryl told me that she was expressing herself more vigorously and sooner than before. She notices that she is not withdrawing from life, and is less concerned about her parents negative reactions to her feelings and wishes. Several months later, Cheryl enrolled in a body movement program, and has been putting on trainings for this type of expressive bodywork.

"Memories" seem to be soul imprints that become patterns or themes in our lives and seem to be pre-programmed to be re-enacted in some form in our present lives. Or perhaps the psyche finds a story to relive that fits with its issues, blocks or patterns. Whether they are seen as psyches' creations, or actual experiences does not seem to matter. The places, events, and people encountered often hold significant meaning for the person. Emotional issues played out in these dramas seem to alleviate the symptom. Perhaps, more importantly, by experiencing the cycle of death, birth and re-birth, we awaken to the world soul. Soul story work, or translife regression pushes back the veil of time wherein we can access our multidimensionality in the collective unconscious of the world psyche.

Archetypal Themes

Soul journeys often embody archetypal themes. Themes of love, abandonment, betrayal, birth and death are examples of the themes that get played out in these real life dramas. Often people are not aware of the archetypal journey or myth they have been living—or has been living them—until they see it in the themes played out before them either in this threshold state of awareness, or in dreams, or distilled from waking-life themes. One of the most amazing aspects of this kind of imaginal process is that changes not only occur in the journeyer's life, but also changes in the lives of people around them. Most all therapists are aware of the domino affect therapy has in the lives of the people around the client when he or she begins to make life changes in their own behavior, relationships and approach to life. But more astounding are these kinds of transformations that occur seemingly as a result of translife regression.

The archetypal motifs, especially death and rebirth tend to unlock the ego's fear of death. People report having a sense of peace knowing or experiencing what seemed to be a re-enactment of very traumatic life endings. Another benefit of this kind of threshold experience is that people begin to see that they have lived many kinds of lives, have been players as antagonists and protagonists. We have been many colors and things. From the humility of finding that once you were the very thing you judge the most—your shadow self for example—your judgments and prejudices of others in the world seem to simply fall away. I remember having untold projection and bias toward Catholicism. I could give so many reasons why I held these prejudices and it was one I knew I would not budge from. Then on one fine day during a regression, I saw myself living the life of a nun! I couldn't believe it, yet there I was in my habit, living a sparse life in another century. From that experience and many others like it, I have retracted my personal judgment and biases. If anything, I have learned that chances are those that I have had any reaction toward are simply mirrors for a traumatic or unresolved life waiting for me to uncover!

Unless these imprints that become patterns or themes are reworked, they seem pre-programmed to be re-enacted in our present lives. By reliving these archetypal motifs in this type of virtual reality, our fixed identities become shattered. These experiences expand the boundaries of the Self. Reliving stories of the soul unlocks patterns at a cellular level and loosens the ego's grip on Maya—the illusion that we are separate from each other and all sentient beings. Soul stories serve to awaken us to the world soul and our connection with one another. It brings humility to our judgments about others and grace to our soul as we begin to understand that we have experienced all things, from rapists, murderers, to heroes and heroines. We begin to find compassion in our heart knowing we have most likely lived in the shoes of the other. "We begin to recognize that our minds are part of an extended web or field of consciousness composed of all the beings that are simultaneously sharing this present moment."[2]

What I am sure of is that this work allows the psyche to "time-travel" to places that exist in the portals of time. It seems as if the Self knows where to go in these psychodramas of the soul. For the past several years I have been studying the effects of this work in people's lives. I have given them a questionnaire, and asked that they wait several months to answer. The reason, of course, is to allow enough time for the person to experience any effects of the regression. The results have continued to astound me.

I once worked with a woman who had psoriasis on her arms and various other places on her body. She came in to look at the origin of her skin disorder, wondering if it had an emotional origin beyond this lifetime. She went back to a life where she was a leper in a leper colony. She had a lover who would visit her there periodically, but she was terrified that he would contract the disease by contact with her, so painfully, she refused to see him. But he insisted on seeing her and did indeed become infected. They lived their lives out there. He died before her and she never forgave herself for killing him. After working with her in the bardo state (the state between lives), where she found self-forgiveness, she was able to understand that her psoriasis was a reflection of her guilt and of holding herself responsible for his death. Several months later she told me that her psoriasis was clearing up, but what she hadn't told me was that she had a son in this lifetime that also had psoriasis. She thought that this son was her lover from the prior incarnation, and that without ever doing anything else, his psoriasis completely cleared up! He knew nothing of her work in regression therapy.

Notwithstanding the possibility that their psoriasis would have cleared up anyway, or that there were other unknown factors, what other conclusions might we make? Could this point to the possibility that time truly is an arbitrary construct and that no matter in what "time" we work on ourselves, we truly are affecting others at the etheric and physical level? I have heard so often after doing this work that current issues with other people clear, without doing anything else. As we work in these fields, we must allow for the idea that we are literally rescripting the conscious mind field because we are working at the *psychoid* levels of psyche. (See Chapter Three for an in-depth discussion of the psychoid.)

Surely the notion of a holographic universe lends credence to the dramas from other times, as well as to this time. I am aware that it is difficult to express these ideas without using the notion of time. I believe that we can use Chronos time—linear time—as a psychological construct to embark upon Soul Journeying, while at the same "time" understanding that the psyche is timeless, and moves with space–time effortlessly. Although referring to "now" and "then," "past" and "future," we must also learn to hold a "neither/nor" position with regard to the nature of the universe, since another view is that all of time is "now."

Transformation in the Imaginal Realms

The changes that have resulted in journeying through the time portals are not always as dramatic as the woman and her son with psoriasis; nevertheless, portals are often major for those who have struggled with patterns in their lives.

A woman I will call "Maria Lena" had a history of migraine headaches. She also had trouble feeling sexual with her husband and wondered why. When I asked her to go back to an unhappy memory in a life, she found herself outside a *pension* in Madrid, Spain. She told me a young South American man, probably 23 years old or so, was accosting her, in a dark, dreary hallway, and she remained emotionless during the rape. Being young herself, and not knowing what else to do, she left the city early the next morning without letting anyone know what had happened to her. Maria Lena reviewed several lives wherein she saw how she remained emotionless in the face of trauma because to do otherwise would threaten her life.

In one of the lives Maria Lena reviewed, she is a Native American woman. She describes herself clearly: "I have plain leather strapped moccasins wrapped around my feet and I am wearing animal skins. I am struck by how plain the moccasins are…no beads or decoration of any kind. My hair is tied back in a loose sort of ponytail and wrapped with leather straps as well. I am carrying a small girl child in a papoose in front of me. I live in a tepee-type structure and am aware that life is extremely hard here. There is a lot of work to do and my hands are rough and worn because of it. I watch as my baby girl looks at me. I realize her life will be difficult as well. I can see some men returning in the distance on horseback carrying some kill of some sort for the tribe."

Asking her to move to the next important scene, she finds herself inside the tepee where a small fire is burning. Her husband enters the tent. She said he was an angry unloving man and wants to take her sexually. "I must submit or I will be hurt. I am aware that this is what I must do, but I clearly do not like it. In fact, I hate it." She is aware that she is pregnant again. She does not wish to have a child if it is a girl, as she is aware that there is no future for her next child as well. She sees that when her daughter is older, age 11 through 13, her husband uses her sexually, too. She tells me she hates him.

In the bardo state she is aware that she made the decision that she would never be treated this way again by a man. She says, though, that perhaps this was one of several lives that helped her to learn to be more assertive and liberated as a woman. She said: "I see how I learned to shut down my feelings. I have a right to my voice. I have a right to decide what will and will not happen to my body. In both lives, I did not allow my feelings to be voiced. In both lives I did things that I felt were wrong but was not strong enough to say this, especially to the men I had to answer to."

Maria Lena told me that prior to the session, she had been having migraine headaches almost every day for about a week. She said that this was extremely unusual as she only had them in times of stress and they never lasted for more than one day. In a follow up with her, Maria Lena told me that her migraines had greatly subsided for months following the one session, and that her libido had increased. Now her migraines occur only with her lunar cycle, "as a reminder of the lesson her body remembers about being a female." Interestingly, Maria Lena's chosen profession is to work with children, many of whom have been sexually molested. She has often found herself in court testifying on the behalf of these children.

Maria Lena's lives are examples of lives that many, many women have had. The memory of rape, molestation, and abuse remains strongly held as an imprint. The other life Maria Lena reviewed was of a Roman soldier and a leader who marched through villages killing women and children. Although she felt many emotions as that soldier and saw that even in them it was dangerous to show human emotions for the pain and grief she—or he—was causing. Maria Lena and Cheryl represent an untold number of people who have lost their voice in the overwhelming traumas that have played throughout history. It is an archetypal imprint that can be seen in translife stories.

Another archetypal theme common in translife stories is one of abandonment. Sheila is such person working through this lifelong theme. The issues of alienation in her life made her feel as though she has never "belonged" to the family into which she was born. Living alone, she longed for a true partner and lover to share her life on the large farm she owns. This feeling of alienation would show up in groups where she has felt different, isolated and unable to relate to others. This had become a pathway to shutting down her heart center, amplifying the problem of feeling disconnected.

In her session, she went to a very ancient time, perhaps "caveman" time. As a young child, she saw that she had wandered away from her clan. Upon returning, she found that everyone had left, leaving her behind. She knew that her clan hadn't realized that she was missing. No one returned for her, and she ended up living alone, fending for herself well into adulthood, a familiar feeling in this life. At her death scene, she saw a pack of wolves waiting hungrily for her to leave her body. In this life, she was still alone.

In another life, a Native American life, Sheila landed in a scene where the white man was attacking and killing her tribe's people. They killed almost everyone, but took a few of the women with them to bring back to the town. She was one of these women. She saw herself obediently living out her life as a maid, along with another woman from her tribe; the only other person she ever saw again from her people. Great sadness and pain overwhelmed her in the session as she saw and relived this. At the same time, she was filled with joy as she recognized the other woman as a dear friend whom she has reconnected with in this life. She was very ready to be leaving that life when I took her to the hour before her death.

At the end of each life, after passing through the threshold into the bardo state (the interlife state), I always ask the person to go to a higher source, and ask what they learned and what they were to have learned from that incarnation. The last thought a person has upon leaving their life gets imprinted and "set" for the next lifetime. In regression work, we can trace that thought and rework it, as it is often an underlying issue or theme in the person's current life. When asking for the soul's purpose, I have found that people are always able to get an answer. Sheila's soul purpose was to learn independence and inner strength. I also like to have people find a lifetime where they had the qualities they long for, an opposite experience so to speak, so that people will have a visceral sense of what that was like.

I directed Sheila to go to a time when she felt that she "belonged." Sheila went to a lifetime in which she was a shaman for a Native American tribe in a later time period. Unlike Maria Lena, upon entering this life she looked down and saw beautifully beaded moccasins on her feet. Her clothing was intricately designed and made with care. She commented that this clothing put Ralph Lauren to shame! She was very powerful and needed by her people. These are her words:

"I loved the experience of the shaman lifetime—to realize how it feels to be totally in my power, and to go easily between worlds, to be different and quite set apart from the rest of the tribe, but at the same time to be respected and honored precisely for my differences. I was a unique person and understood my role and accepted it fully. I believe this is a key for me now, in order to gain mastery at being in this world but not of it."

Sheila found that after this regression, she felt a huge shift in her life. The block or holding pattern as she called it suddenly melted away. She felt much more creative energy. The fear of "coming out of the closet" as a healer led her to write an article about her healing work, which simultaneously advertised her work for business. She said that suddenly she felt much more confident and inspired. After the session, Sheila said she also felt ready to be in a relationship. Recently I heard that she had met a man that she was "crazy" about.

I want to emphasize that sometimes, issues are so long-standing and deep that one Holographic Journey is not enough to release all the webs that are interwoven in the pattern. Sometimes several sessions are needed to trace back to all the "origins."

For two years I met with my teacher, Whitecloud, and journeyed to past times, unlocking blocks and patterns in my life that only made sense after seeing and reliving the dramas. I experienced many lives, and met many of the players who are presently in my life. I was able to see the workings and the reason I chose parents this time where part of my soul's lessons came through child abuse. I saw my part in the overall drama and was freed from my pain, not to mention years of psychotherapy!

One soul journey I entered one year brought about an instant release of a curious idiosyncrasy. All of my life I had this strange attraction to fires. I was both repelled and attracted to them. If I saw one, I had an overwhelming desire to go to where it was burning. None of this made sense to me, as I had never had any traumatic events with a fire. I had never seen one up close nor had I been in one. On one occasion, I was driving to Whitecloud's rather remote place in the hills of Northern California. It was late summer, when the foothills are baked dry, and fires are always a threat. Over the trees, I saw a plume of smoke rising above the hill in the direction I was driving. Driving to Whitecloud's place each month always put me in a quasi-trance. On this occasion, I became so entranced with the fire that I got hopelessly lost. When I woke from my daze, I couldn't tell where I was on this particular windy, back road. It was before the advent of cellular phones, so all I could do was to turn around and retrace my steps. Finally, I recognized a bend in the road and made it to my mentor's sacred spot.

Already in an altered state when the session began, I immediately saw myself in a prairie-like field, and I was running toward my burning log cabin home. I knew that my two children were in that house. I had been out early in the morning gathering herbs, and somehow I knew that my husband, a fur-trader, was away from home. By the time I got back to the small rustic cabin, it was too late; it was ablaze as I fell to the ground screaming for my children, who died in the fire. I do not remember how I died in that life, but I remember the terror of seeing that fire. Now here is the amazing thing about it: never once since reliving that so-called memory have I ever been plagued by the strange "push-pull" feeling with fires. Whatever else that life was about, the reason for my terror of fires was fully lived and released.

Soul journeys seem to have shamanic-like features. A person enters an altered state, and begins to travel through a portal, landing in the perfect life mirroring the problem, which begins to take on a life of its own. Like a split-screen television, not only do you watch the story unfold, but also you relive it at the same time. As the facilitator, the remarkable thing is that I am able to "see" the scenes as they unfold along with the journeyer. All I need are a couple of identifying details, and I am instantly there as well. Sometimes as I am watching,

97

I can see what has happened before the person realizes it. For example, I may see a sword in a person's shoulder. I am careful not to ask, "Is there a sword in your shoulder?" but rather, "what is happening with your shoulder?" And even less leading: "is there anything happening in your body?" Almost always the journeyer confirms what I have seen. Sometimes, as a person tells me the details of their clothing; not only do I clearly see them, but a time period also emerges along with a sense of the place. This allows me to ask more questions, helping the journeyer to become even more immersed in the scene as it plays out. Often people will resist seeing how they died, leaving their bodies before it has succumbed to physical death. I will see the way a person dies, and will know that great pain remains at the cellular level, although they left the body as it died to avoid the terror and pain. At this point in regression work, the pain needs to be addressed to release the somatic imprint.

Here is the story of a 37-year-old man, I will call Hans, who came to me because of a physical reaction he had every time he tried to meditate. Hans was from Austria, and had been in the states for several years. He worked as an editor for a large national magazine. He told me he was a prolific reader, and had read several books on past-life regression. Because he said he had tried many other therapies to resolve this problem, and none of them worked, he thought maybe this kind of therapy might help him. He had tried several years of traditional psychotherapy, had been to body workers—which he said had a profound impact on him—but had actually brought this emotion up in his body even stronger. It had reached a level where it was interfering in his life every day. He had given up on his meditation practice, even though he did not want to.

Here is how he described the problem: "When I relax, a very strong fear is coming up, while I relax into it and try not to resist it, it grows steadily stronger (until I resist it). It is a fear of destruction—annihilation. Combined with it is a strong feeling of grief, resignation, terror and a feeling of something strangling my neck, and I actually start to cough while feeling nauseous until it gets too strong for me and I start to resist it, and then it submerges." Hans went on to say that it happened now *every* time he tried to relax. He could remember the sensation the first time as far back as 16 years old.

I usually lead people in a relaxation exercise before doing an induction. Because the issue was that Hans couldn't relax, almost immediately when I asked him to breathe deeply and relax, the block in his body came up. He began choking, coughing and grabbing his chest. He seemed to be in great fear, and started screaming "NO! NO!" while writhing on the sofa. He went directly into a life where he was being beaten to death by a group of men in uniforms. After being killed in a brutal attack, I asked him what had happened. Still crying, he emphatically stated: "I didn't betray them—I didn't!" I am innocent!! And after a moment, "I want to kill them!!"

In taking him back over the scene, he described the men in uniforms, having beige coats with black belts and helmets on their heads. He said he was 23 years old and it was in England in 637 A.D. He was a commander of some kind and was accused of betraying someone. The Tibetans have said that at the moment of death—and birth—that crucial life decisions are made and imprinted throughout our lives until somehow it is retrieved and released. Stan Grof's holotropic breathwork takes people back to their birth where one's whole life's template is inscribed on the psyche. Core beliefs such as "it's not safe to be here," or "I have to work hard to live," or "I give up," are a few examples of core beliefs that are set in the moments just before and after birth. The same is true in death. The decision, or belief a person had becomes locked in the body as well as the psyche. This is why it is vital to track a person's belief about themselves or their lives at the moment after crossing the threshold of life or death.

In Hans's case, he wanted revenge; he was angry to have had his young life so brutally and abruptly taken from him, as are many lives in translife regressions. One of the ways to help a person have some objectivity about the situation is to take the person into the bardo realm and work from the place of spirit. I suggested to Hans to go to the place between lives and told him he could call forth those men to be able to tell them how he felt about their betrayal of him. After the men gathered there, he said to them: "I was innocent! How could you do this to me, I was helping you! Why? Why? It was not fair!" He told me they said that they were only doing their jobs, and then he saw that he was also involved in a form of political intrigue, and he was the scapegoat. Someone more powerful then he ordered his death. He saw that he "set people up" to die as well, saying, "I played a smart game and someone outsmarted me…but I felt so righteous, you know?"

Taking him to a higher source or Self, I asked him to find out what he was to have learned in that lifetime. Immediately he "heard" forgiveness. I took him through several more life stories connected to the fear and emotion in his chest. In one life drama, he was hung to death, but struggled valiantly before dying. In another drama he relived the life of a lieutenant in World War II. He died being shot in the upper chest after giving the command to kill many others. After reliving this death, he said that he felt horrible remorse, that he didn't do the right thing. He said that he was always fascinated by war movies, but always felt sad and cried when seeing the battle scenes, feeling that war was such a waste, so senseless. I asked him if he thought that the remorse he felt then as a soldier was still with him in his life now. At this, he began to weep, saying yes, he "feels so ashamed." He learned from his Higher Self the soul lessons in that life were to let go of the need for power and that he needed to find self-forgiveness. He learned that he needed these experiences of war and killing in order to value life and the lives of others. He said he could see that he still needed to let go of the desire for power. What a wonderful lesson!

I asked him to see if there was a lifetime when he was powerful, but was not abusing his power. After a minute he could see himself wearing a long grayish robe, "with something about the waist, and over one shoulder, like a priest or something," he said with his Austrian accent, while gesturing with his hands. "I have dark, curly hair, sandals…it feels like Ancient Greece." At the same moment, I could see him standing on marble steps—with lots of marble pillars in the background. He felt like he might have been a very wise man, very sure of himself, yet humble.

I asked him, "It looks as if there is lots of marble around, like you are standing on huge steps outdoors?"

"Yes! Yes! It is like I am a philosopher of some sort, lots of wisdom. I do what I loved, my people like me and respect me, and it is an easy life." Later Hans reflected that perhaps he was too complacent and needed those later lives to learn more soul lessons. However reviewing this Greek life gave him much comfort, and he saw that he had brought his philosopher part with him into this life.

What was even better was that Hans said later that a shift had taken place. He was excited because he no longer had the strong feelings in his body when he relaxed. The following day, he said he still had a slight residue left in his body, but nothing like before. My sense was that after a while it would be completely gone. For a person like Hans, one session may not be nearly enough to clear old patterns and themes. Often, three or four sessions are needed to follow all the threads karmically tied to a physical or emotional response, pattern or theme.

I also want to point out that it is always important to medically rule out any physical etiology when someone has physical symptoms. Hans had been to several physicians to address the underlying problem and none were found. In addition, holographic or past life regressions are not a "cure all" for present day problems and issues in need of traditional kinds of psychotherapies.

Exercise #2

Holographic Journeying

Although this is more difficult to do without being guided, it is still possible and I know many people who have had many "past-life" recalls using this method. It is not very different from the other kinds of interactive imagery exercises that I give you in the following chapter.

First, find a place where you can lie down and become relaxed with a good amount of undisturbed time. After deep breathing and grounding, set your intention to find the origin of an issue you have struggled with or a pattern in your life that continues to haunt you. Next, move into the feeling of it in your body. What does it feel like? Ask your self "what is this like?"

Wait for a feeling or an image or a knowing about it to emerge. For example, you might say, "this heaviness in my chest feels like a huge weight is on top of me." What is that like? Wait for an image to form, and then see what happens next. Next look down at your feet, see what your feet have on them. Next look at your clothing. What images come up, what senses do you have about the time period?

Ask what happens next once you are in your imagery. Follow it with this question, all the way to and through your death. This will be an interesting experience and you may feel like you are making it up. That is okay. Allow our psyche to make up whatever story it wants to make up about the problem or issue you set your intention to look at.

Give yourself the suggestion that you will remember this and feel refreshed after you come fully back. Know that you may also have more spontaneous "memories." As soon as you feel complete, record this in your journal for reference later.

Chapter Five

Behind the Veil

The Caterpillar and Alice looked at each other for
some time in silence: at last the Caterpillar took the
hookah out of its mouth, and addressed her in a
languid, sleepy voice.
"Who are you?" said the Caterpillar.
Alice replied rather shyly, "I—I hardly know, Sir, just
at present—at least I know who I was when I got up
this morning, but I think I must have been changed
several times since then."
"What do you mean by that?" said the Caterpillar,
sternly. "Explain yourself!"

> -Lewis Carroll *Alice in Wonderland*

Guidance from Within

I have found that people open to multiple dimensions and multiple
possibilities while in an altered state. When we enter an interactive
field or an imaginal realm there are many fields with accompanying
vibratory patterns that can be accessed. Often when I direct people to
an inner resource, such as to their Oversoul or Higher Self, and invite
them to ask what their soul purpose is, I am always amazed at the
answers people receive. I also direct them to ask any question that
they may have for this inner "Philemon," or resource.

103

Always, people are able to receive answers that seem to come as an awareness that they previously did not have. When I ask them to tell me what they heard or learned, I often get chills—the visceral response I have when touched by the sacred. These moments seem to light up, stand out, and feel very real to me and to the journeyer. I do not know how this works, or what allows this resourceful guidance from within, or from elsewhere. I do know that everyone I have ever asked has been able to hear vivid responses from this source. Tapping into this wisdom has always been helpful and transformative for people. Ultimately, the purpose of this work is to bring transformation and self-awareness into our lives. Tapping into this core essence requires a quieting of the mind, and a shift of awareness. It is through a meditative mind that we can shift into a finer frequency to be able to hear the voices of the divine. It is the door through which we can hear the words of our soul source.

Another way into the inner world of resources is through imagery. Guiding people into a realm where their own guidance lives is a wonderful tool for listening to the inner wisdom that resides there. In this imaginal realm we can meet our inner guides, ask for gifts, open doors to places that have been inaccessible yet reveal important information for the journey ahead. In the last chapter, I will give you keys to access your own inner guidance.

Exercise #3

Interactive Imagery

This exercise is useful to gain information for yourself. First decide what it is that you would want to know. Get comfortable, and begin breathing deeply. Notice your body—how it feels. Ground your energy into the Earth (for a detailed exercise on grounding, see Chapter Six, p.119). Now allow an image of a place out of doors to appear. As you look around, you will see a mansion in the near distance. Begin to walk up to it and you will see stairs that lead you up to the front door. Walk up the stairs and let yourself in through the large door. Now you will see a hallway in the foyer. In the hallway, there will be three doors. One represents the past, one represents the present, and one represents the future. Wait until you know which door wants you to open it. You will get a definite impression of which door it is. When you are ready open it, the answer will be waiting for you in some form. You may see a guide who will tell you the answer, or you will get a clear image of what the answer is. After you have your information return to the hallway. You will now see a round table in the foyer and on it will be a gift for you. Take this gift and open it. Allow yourself to understand its meaning.

* * *

Often in these interactive imageries people are given gifts they don't want. Our inner judgments and resistances are unrelentingly mirrored back to us in these imageries. I remember one woman in a weekend seminar I gave on developing intuition who was given a dead cat. She recoiled at the gift and didn't want to take it. The members of the group wouldn't accept her refusal of the gift. When she explored this image further, she discovered that she had not been taking care of her body and its needs. The cat was a symbol of the instinctual self, or chi that had been disregarded and was crying for attention. It was the most important gift she could have received from her inner guidance as it could save her life. Another woman came to a door in the imagery. When she stood in front of the door she had an urge to open it but didn't want to see what was inside. She opened it, and found dead bodies piled high, reminiscent of the archetypal myth of "Bluebeard." With this door opened she began to see that she had work to do, or "things to look at that she didn't want to see."

The gifts received are not always understood. You must trust that the gift is of value and must not be discarded. Many times I have seen people in these journeys receive gifts of precious stones, emeralds or diamonds that await the inner traveler.

Listening to Your Dreams

In Chapter Two, I talked about how dreams are gateways into the personal and collective psyche. I shared how dreams have played an important part of our history and how other cultures regard them as dimensions worthy of living their daytime lives via the import of the dream message.

I explained that dreams are not only gateways to the personal unconscious but are also thresholds to the cosmic world soul. Dreams are a significant resource for your inner guidance. This chapter focuses on inner direction and ways to access it. Dreams are of vital importance for daily contact with your inner guidance. I know many persons who rely on their dream life to guide them in waking life. Our dream life comes unfettered by the waking ego and therefore has a greater chance of being from an "objective" resource, meaning that dreams can come from varied multidimensional realms.

The following dream is one that gave me a "peek" into the year ahead and felt like guidance for what was to come.

I am painting a "set" for a play or production. It is an oblong set and I am spray painting the floor. As I spray, it comes out a golden checkerboard pattern. The back part of the set isn't finished so I go back there and begin painting the walls in green. I recognize that I can see what needs to be done and I just do it without being told what's next.

This dream presented itself to me on my birthday and I entitled it "New Productions." I felt that in the dream I was getting ready for a "new play"—or perhaps a new way to play in life. I had the feeling that the play was something like *Alice in Wonderland*. I associate *Alice in Wonderland* with being in altered states of consciousness, just the very thing I like to play in. The back part of the set could be my unconscious, the part that still needs work. I know what I have to do and do it; this knowing feels like "resolve" or an understanding of what I need to do to make the next step in my journey. The color green makes me think of new life, new growth. The golden checkerboard I associate with a chess game, the game of life. Because the checkerboard is golden, the dream tells me I am on the right path.

Dreams are a resource that can be a guide not only for our outer world life but also for the meaning of our psychological processes as seen in my birthday dream. These dreams can be extremely helpful in giving us a look at what is happening in the personal unconscious realm of our psyche of which we are not otherwise aware. When I remember that Jung said, "An uninterpreted dream is like an unopened letter from God," it is for me a motivating factor for understanding my psyche's dream language.

Jung, whose work branched away from Freud's in the early 1900s, said that dreams come from the unconscious, both the personal unconscious and the collective, believing some dream images have a universal meaning. Jung noticed that imagery from the unconscious is often replicated in the images from alchemy, fairytales and myth, and therefore have a universal meaning that he termed archetypal. For example, in my opening dream, gold has a universal or archetypal meaning of something that is precious, important, and often has a spiritual sense to it. Gold in alchemy was the opus metal, one that represented the ultimate evolution of the Self.

Our unconscious has a greater understanding of ourselves than does our waking ego, therefore the dream psyche or unconscious is not hampered by the ego and its judgments during sleep states. Dreams often mirror back to us something that we were not "aware" of in the ego (waking) state. The psyche has an automatic healing response and will try to balance what is out of balance. Therefore, dreams will often be compensatory, meaning that they will compensate for a waking attitude that may be out of balance with our greater Self.

Dreams are not only important for the life of an individual but represent parts of an immense "web of destiny," which pertain to all of humanity. Dreams have always been an important part of history. In times past, they have been used as oracles and divination. At the turn of the 19th century, Freud began looking at dreams as a way to see into the unconscious drives of the personal unconscious, while Jung saw them as pointing outward toward universal motifs and archetypes in the collective unconscious. Both realized that dreams performed a meaningful function in the lives of their patients and they began using them as tools in analysis toward transformation and individuation.

Today there are many books written on dream interpretation. These books offer ways to understand and use dreams for personal growth. I have worked with dreams for many years in dream circles and in individual therapy with my clients. In my own life, I can't even imagine not looking at the meaning of my dreams as inner guidance and help from a rich inner resource. As I stated earlier, the wonderful thing about dreams is that they come from an unadulterated source, a source without the ego's influence.

I have many examples of dreams that have guided others in their lives and many of them have led to major life changes. A couple of them in particular have led these persons to making important decisions in their life. Dreams may also bring information with regard to a problem you are struggling with. For example, our "ego" self may want to do something our unconscious "knows" would be a poor choice. I remember one woman in particular who was looking at houses to buy. She found one she really liked and "incubated" a dream (asked the psyche to give her a dream) to get some guidance on whether the house she found was a good house for her to buy. It was a house that she really liked and, of course, she wanted a dream confirming her choice. Instead, she got a dream that showed her a house with windows that were falling off, cracks in the wall and dark spots on the ceiling. Still not satisfied with this answer, she asked again for another dream about the house. This time she got a dream in which the living room was filled with laundry and it was hard to find a place to walk without things strewn everywhere. In interpreting the dream, she felt the laundry indicated that there would be a lot of work and upkeep, which was also the feeling in the dream. As a result, she did not opt to buy the house, and instead purchased another. Later, she found out that the house she almost bought did indeed have quite a few structural problems that were not evident in the walkthrough.

Another dreamer had a dream that told her to get out of her job. She was working for several years in a children's cancer center, facilitating a comprehensive care program for families, a program she herself developed. This dream woke her up to the fact that she was burnt out from the weekly deaths of her child patients. Here is the dream:

I dreamed that I was in the trenches in World War I, somewhere in Germany. I was a medic who brought in the wounded and dying on a stretcher. I was aware that the other person at the end of the stretcher was killed, discharged, or kept returning to America and I had to keep finding a replacement to help me. Finally, I knew that if stayed in this job, it would kill me, but suddenly I knew I could serve at home. With this thought I became elated in the dream and woke up.

Immediately she knew that she too could leave. She realized that she needed to quit her job and that it was okay to do so. At the time she was actually living in California and "going to America," for her, represented going to a place she felt at home. She knew it was the decision she wasn't allowing herself to even think about due to guilt about leaving the families in her care. This is one of those dreams that bring a sudden realization to underlying feelings, which sometimes are just beyond the periphery of awareness.

It is a bit disconcerting when dreams and reality meet. Annie, another person I was working with, had a dream in which she was standing on the shore and saw a dying fisherman in a boat. There was a cat in the boat perched on the edge meowing frantically to get her attention. She was aware in the dream that she did not want to have to rescue the man in the boat. He was out in the middle of the water and she would have to swim out to the boat. In the dream she did not know what to do and was feeling frustrated that the cat wouldn't allow her to keep walking.

In waking life, this woman had just left a long-term relationship. The morning of her dream she told me she had found a photo on the Internet that her ex-partner had sent to her. Synchronistically, it was of a man in a boat in a bay of water! She said there was no note or explanation as to why he sent the picture. She felt the dream was speaking of her dying relationship and the cat in her dream wanted her to rescue this man. To me this wasn't quite "it." Why would this cat be so insistent? I asked her if she would mind entering the dream and seeing where it took her. After reentering the imagery she again felt the cat's urgency and her reluctance to go out there.

I asked, "What happens next?"

She told me the cat turned into a being, like a human, but still cat-like. Annie felt that she couldn't just leave the man there so she goes out to the boat. She still doesn't want to rescue him. In her imagery, she begins to pull the boat to shore where a beautiful light shines down upon them. She says he is dying and maybe he needs to die. I ask her to follow the imagery and see what happens next.

Next she is in the boat with the dying man and she feels it would be all right to allow him to put his head against her shoulder. She tells me she can feel energy moving into him through her and he begins to feel better. The cat nearby seems consoled by this new energy. Annie tells me that the cat is now on her lap and it is giving her energy as well. She feels the presence of the other being of light nearby. Finally, she feels ready to allow herself to experience this old man as a part of herself.

Annie readily looks at the meaning of the dream in a "new light." She realized that her work was to heal her own inner masculinity. In her life, she had been in a series of relationships where she was trying to "fix" the outer man, and invariably, this became an unsatisfactory way of relating for her and her partner. This "dying man" in the dream represented a part of her own wounded self and in the most beautiful way Psyche led her to the true inner healing that comes from being open to inner guidance. In waking life, Annie loves cats and I thought it was interesting that one of her beloved animals became the animal guide that led her to what she needed for her inner growth and transformation.

We can see that dreams come in many forms of guidance. Sometimes they focus on the inner process we are in, and sometimes they give concrete direction for the next step of the journey in waking life. Always, dreams are a reliable resource that never lie. It is our work to learn to open the dream and read what meaning the dream images have for us for guidance and support.

It is always important to honor the dream by doing something in the outer world to concretize it. Jung often asked his patients what they were going to do to honor the dream and made sure they followed through with their offering back to the dream psyche by doing concrete, outer world things such as painting the dream.

Exercise #4

Embodying Dream Work

Once you have a dream written down, there are several techniques you can use to better understand your dream. First begin with asking yourself questions about the dream. In dream work, there is a premise that all parts of the dream are parts of you or represent parts of you. Begin with the feeling of the dream: How were you feeling in the dream? How were you feeling when you woke up? I suggest writing these answers in your dream journal. Next, identify the parts of the dream. Who are the players in the dream? If you dreamed of a person you know, ask what qualities does this person have. What are your associations to this person? What is this person like?

For example, if you dream of your boss, answer the above questions. If you answer that this person is critical of you most of the time, ask what part of you is like this. What part of you is criticizing you for something you are doing? How do you feel about this?

Next you will be bridging these answers to something that feels similar to this in your everyday life. So the question would be: "What is going on in my life now that feels like I am being criticized?" Usually dreams reflect a feeling about something currently going on. People often will have dreams about circumstances or people form the past. It may seem unrelated until you remember what the feeling in your life was at that time, or the feeling around that circumstance in your past. Once you ask yourself if this feels anything like something happening in my life today, you may then get a big "aha." The "aha" is a response that you actually feel throughout your body. When leading dream groups, everyone can feel it when someone has this experience.

Gayle Delaney has authored several books on dreams and uses pragmatic questions to deliver the "aha" feeling that comes from getting the meaning of your dream correct. Although there are volumes of dream books on the market that are excellent, I like to refer people to Living Your Dreams as a place to begin with dream interpretation.

* * *

Philemon: Inner Guide or Otherworld Phenomenon?

How does the world of the ancestors play a part in the imaginal realms? Through the many portals in the imaginal realm we are able to contact the Otherworld where the "Invisibles," or the ancestral realms, exist. From what perspective do we acknowledge the Invisibles? Jung referred to the ancestors as the Invisibles, which are also sometimes referred to as discarnate entities in metaphysical writing. According to these metaphysical traditions, these Invisibles are present within the imaginal realm, yet they exist independently within it and we are able to make contact through it.

It was through active imagination that Jung met Philemon, an Otherworld, other-time being, although Jung seemed to vacillate between his understanding of Philemon as a sub-personality from the unconscious, or a separate spiritual entity. Philemon began to appear to him and speak with him regularly when Jung systematically entered the process of active imagination. Philemon "taught him more about the unconscious than any of the other figures he encountered in the unconscious. Philemon, was in short, a spiritual guru, exactly similar to those found in India, but at least fifteen years before Jung had any idea of their existence of the latter."[1] Many years later, Jung felt validated regarding Philemon when he learned that most East Indians had a living guru, but some had spirits for their teachers.[2]

Although Jung honored his dreams as paramount to the reality of any situation, Jung was ambivalent about the certainty of reincarnation even though he had been to India and had studied with yogis. Jung has been accused of not understanding the psyche beyond the notion of individuation, meaning that he did not understand the nature of enlightenment. He did, however, question the notion of the continuity of soul, or the Self beyond death. He raised an important question as to whether we are a personal continuity of Self, or a matrix of experiences including those of our ancestors. In his autobiography, *Memories, Dreams and Reflections*, Jung states:

> The crucial question is whether a man's karma is personal or not. If it is, then preordained destiny with which a man enters life represents an achievement of previous lives, and a personal continuity therefore exists. If, however, this is not so, and an impersonal karma is seized upon in the act of birth, then that karma is incarnated again without there being any personal continuity... I know no answer to the question of whether the karma which I live is the outcome of my past lives, or whether it is not rather the achievement of my ancestors, whose heritage comes together in me. Am I a combination of the lives of these ancestors and do I embody these lives again? Have I lived before in the past as a specific personality, and did I progress so far in that life that I am now able to seek a solution? I do not know. Buddha left the question open, and I like to assume that he himself did not know with certainty.[3]

Some who knew Jung privately have said that he leaned toward the notion of the validity of reincarnation near the end of his life. It is easy to see from the above quote that Jung left the possibility open that Philemon could have been an ancestor or other-life personality.

Jung was not unfamiliar with psychic phenomena either. In fact, his first paper was written from his research into the occult. In Barbara Hannah's biography of Jung, she wrote that in Jung's life at Bollingen, his home in Switzerland, he thought of himself as having two personalities. Quoting from his autobiography, *Memories, Dreams and Reflections*, Jung emphasized that his home at Bollingen, was primarily the home of his No. 2 personality—Philemon—"that timeless or eternal figure in man which yet needs the No.1 personality" to experience three-dimensional reality and the here and now in this moment of time."[4] He told Hannah that at Bollingen he was in his true life, while in the personality of Philemon, who existed outside of time. Hannah revealed that Jung did most of his writing "out of the No. 2 personality," and that Jung disliked unannounced visits to his home because he was so thoroughly entrenched in his No. 2 personality.[5]

I believe that Jung was actually connecting with an autonomous being from the collective unconscious or the world soul. Perhaps Philemon was an ancestor, or soul aspect of himself from the future, like in author Robert Monroe's trilogy, *Journeys Out of the Body, Far Journeys,* and *Ultimate Journey*. In this series, Monroe meets a being that called himself the "I-there" which turned out to be an Oversoul aspect of himself from his future. (Robert Monroe is renowned for his out-of-body studies at the Monroe Institute in Virginia Beach, Virginia,). In any case, Philemon was an inner guide that provided Jung with a rich inner resource for his life.

What Jung said of Philemon is what the shamen have always known: "Philemon brought home to me the crucial insight that there are things in the psyche which I do not produce, which produce themselves and have their own life. Philemon taught Jung a most significant and profound lesson when he said to him that he [Jung] mistakenly 'treated thoughts as if [he] generated them,' and in contrast to this view Philemon said to Jung, 'thoughts were like animals in the forest, or people in a room, or birds in the air.' Philemon then added, 'if you should see people in a room, you would not think that you had made those people or that you were responsible for them.'"[6] From this teaching, Jung truly learned the autonomy of the psyche in which Jung admitted to learning most of what he wrote. Jung said that Philemon taught him many things and he had many conversations with him on a wide variety of subjects. We don't know if Philemon was an actual person from another time, an ancestor, or even Jung himself from a previous incarnation! Nevertheless, Philemon, it seems to me, was truly an "Other" world visitor that came to Jung not unlike many inner guides who come from other dimensions, or those who are disembodied spirit guides.

Philippe of the Knight's Templar

Portals into the mystic realms come in many forms. As we have seen in Chapter Four, one of these portals is through holographic or soul journeys. Holographic journeys seem to amplify our connectedness via the web of life. They also bring guidance and transformation into our lives. Some regressionists have thought that it is possible to go back in time and rework the events of the "past" so that the events of the "future" travel a path on a higher vibrational level. There is a hot debate about the ethical implications of this kind of work in regressionist journals. I am not sure where I stand with the ethical implications, but I have had people "re-work" many soul story endings to feel benefited by that work. However, in this next story, I felt no need to change what was presenting itself.

A physician called me to explore the reason why she was having a very unusual experience. Jennie felt that journeying into a "past-life" might reveal some answers. Jennie began her story by showing me a scar that ran from her forehead down the side of her face. Not evident at first, but with a closer look, it was visible under makeup.

Jennie told me that she was born with a birthmark on the right side of her face. When she was a teen, she decided to have it removed. The doctor assured her that there would be no scar, but in fact it did scar, leaving a small one-inch slash down the right side of her temple. Then, several months prior to seeing me, she had been walking a horse back to its barn when it reared landing a hoof smack in the middle of her forehead. With blood spurting out of the gash, she was rushed to emergency and was given several stitches.

Now barely visible, she was wondering about this scar because of a vision she had had at a workshop. At the end of the day in her workshop with Drunvalo Melchizedek, author of the *Flower of Life* volumes, and teacher of sacred geometry among other things, Melchizedek had their group of twelve lying head to head in a circular fashion while leading them in meditation. Jennie told me that they went into a deep altered state. Later that evening in her room as she was lying on the bed still in an altered state, suddenly, she saw a man standing at the end of her bed. He was wearing a suit of "mail" and clearly seemed to want to speak to her. She asked him who he was. He said his name was Philippe of the Knights Templar. He told Jennie that he was *she* in another time! Before she could ask anything else he disappeared. Uncannier for her was the fact that he had a large scar that ran down the right side of his face—exactly as her scars now appeared on her face. This was what brought her into the session—

she wanted to know who Philippe was and how she was connected to him.

I took Jennie into a state of relaxation as usual, and then asked her to go into a life time that would give her more information about this scar she had acquired and Philippe. She "landed" first in the life of a monk in the 1600s in France.

She said, "I am walking down a narrow hallway with high arches."

"What do you have on?" I ask, as I saw a man in a long robe made of rough fabric. The archways seemed rather tall and seemed to be made of wood and plaster.

"I have on a long robe, that ties over the shoulder. I am a monk, and I am going to the garden to pray."

"Okay, move to the next important thing."

"I am having a vision, I see a crucifix with a dove." Jennie's face looked beatific at this point as I saw the monk kneeling in the garden, looking upward in prayer. I wanted to see his vision as well but was unable to do so. The monk seemed ecstatic, as I quietly waited so as not to intrude on her/his ecstatic experience.

Jennie said she loved that life and her work in that life, and saw that her job was to record ancient esoteric wisdom for future generations. At the end of her life, she said that the king had ordered that they be killed as heretics, and she, along with the other monks, were hung alive on a stake to die. I asked her to tell me what she was experiencing at the moment of death. She practically shouted as she saw her "brethren" all around her. She said she felt blissful to be free of her body and to be able to join Christ with her brothers. I asked her if she knew any of them from this life. After a pause, she said, "yes," there was one man who had been her uncle in this life. As she said this, I saw a rotund man with balding hair, sitting at a desk with a quill pen in his hand. After the session, I asked her about him, and she confirmed that this described him well in that life.

The next life in which she found herself was that of Philippe— in France once again. She said that he was one of the Knights Templar, and he had dedicated his life to protecting esoteric knowledge. As Philippe, she had become conscious of being in a field outside and was praying. Philippe said, "I often come here to commune with those teaching and guiding me from the other realms." I could see a structure of some sort on a knoll not too far away. It looked like it was partially built in a Normandy-style castle, yet it didn't seem to be a castle. I was puzzled and asked if there was a structure of some sort there in the distance. "Yes," she replied, "that is where we live and preserve the Sacred Wisdom."

"Who lives there?" I asked.

"The Knights Templar."

In the next scene, she/he is in a round room inside the castle, or monastery.

"There are twelve arched windows with symbols in an alcove with stained glass." As she described the scene, I was able to see these windows and the room. It was lined in old stone, like a tower room. Each arched window was rather small yet held a symbol that corresponded to the stone slab. She/he then tells me that there are twelve slabs of stone each with a symbol, lying head to head in a circle, and there is one Knight on each slab. In the middle of the circle there is some sort of crystal. The Knights in her imagery are in deep meditation and the stone is lit up, and they lying in the same circular fashion just as she was in her workshop with Drunvalo. As I watch I see a large flame or light rising up into the middle of the room, pulsating. The Knights are on their backs on the stones, and appear to be in an altered state. Philippe tells me that they are in communion with an Otherworld dimension, a world of a higher vibration where this knowledge is being retained. He is told that the esoteric knowledge that he holds would have to go underground and that it would be brought forth at another time through the feminine. Philippe is also told that the current ruler, who is afraid of the ancient knowledge that they hold, will kill them.

In the next scene, the king's army is storming the castle. The Knights are in their mail suits of armor, and even though they know the outcome, they fight to preserve their lives and perhaps the esoteric knowledge to which they had dedicated their lives. Philippe is killed with the blow of a sword across his forehead and down the side of his face. After death, he said that he felt that he had done his job well and had no regrets.

In the bardo state, I asked Philippe what he wanted of Jennie, and why he had come to her. She told me he said that he wanted her to bring back the esoteric teachings. I ask her to ask how is she to do this. Jennie replies, "I don't know." At that moment, I see a quill pen made of gold light being handed to her. I tell her what I see and she begins to cry. Jennie is the author of a book on women's issues but has not written on esoteric subjects. I believe she has much more writing to do...

After this session, Jennie told me that she had always loved France, and had visited there many times. She felt she was familiar with the part of the country where these lives had taken place and had special fondness for the land there but never knew why. Now she felt she knew what had drawn her there so many times.

I had not known anything about the Knights Templar. In researching the history of the Knights Templar, I found that they originated in France in the early 1100s. "They were said to have been established by a group of nine French knights, who took vows of poverty, chastity and obedience and swore to protect the Holy Land."[7] Some accounts record the Knights Templar as safeguarding the highways for pilgrims. However, Laurence Gardner, author of *Bloodline of the Holy Grail,* states that it is highly inconceivable that nine knights could follow through with such an enormous obligation. In truth, Gardner says, there was a great deal more to the order. The Bishop of Chartres wrote about the Templars as early as 1114, calling them the *Milice du Christi*: Soldiers of Christ.[8] At that time the Knights were already living in King Baldwin II du Bourg's palace, which was located in a mosque on the site of "King Solomon's Temple." When King Baldwin moved to the Tower of David, the temple quarters were left entirely to the Order of Templars. Perhaps this is why I saw the structure like a castle but not a castle. It was more of a temple!

The Knights were a very select group. "They were sworn to a particular oath of obedience—not to the king, nor to their leader, but to their Cistercian Abbot, St Bernard de Clairvaux, who died in 1153."[9] Bernard is known as the saint who rescued Scotland's failing Celtic Church, and rebuilt the Columbian monastery on the Isle of Iona in Scotland, known as the place where the Book of Kells originated. The Knights of the Order were hand-picked by St. Bernard, and they included Archambaud de Saint Amand, Geoffrey Bisol, Rosal, Gondemare, Godefroi, Payen de Montidideir, and

Phillipe d'Alsace, (*Italics added*) the Comte de Flandres, to whom the French author, Chrétien de Troyes' 12th-centrury work, *Le Conte del Graal*, was dedicated.[10] Gardner writes, "Grail lore was born directly out of this early Templar environment, and the *Perlesvaus* portrayed the Knights as the wardens of a great and sacred secret."[11]

I do not know if this was the same Philippe that Jennie relived. The Knights Templar were a sacred order for several hundred years. Also, Jennie stated that there were twelve knights in her order. So this may have been another Philippe in a later time period, or Philippe again in another life as a knight. In my research I found that the knowledge that was once revered was indeed what caused their persecution by the Dominicans of the 14th century Inquisition, where they were killed because of the privileged information they held concerning sacred geometry and Universal Law, just as Jennie foresaw in her Holographic Journey.[12] I do not know the extent to which Jennie knew of the Knights Templar and if all this information was contained in her personal unconscious. I do know that for me there was an uncanny fitting of the facts when I researched her story.

Another oddity I came across was said to be one of the greatest mysteries of Cistercian Gothic architecture. It is the *stained glass* used in the cathedral windows! It appeared in the early 12th century, but disappeared just as suddenly in the middle of the 13th century. "Nothing like it had ever been seen before, and nothing like it has been seen since. It was said to be able to retain its luminosity whether it was bright outside or not. Even in twilight, this glass retained its brilliance way beyond that of any other."[13] Scientists have been unable to replicate the unique power the stained glass had, which was to convert harmful ultraviolet rays into beneficial light. It was said that the adept's [alchemist's] method of staining the glass incorporated the *Spiritus Mundi*—"the cosmic breath of the universe."[14]

Exercise #5

Meeting an Inner Guide

Set your intention to meet an inner guide. Once again find a place to relax. Breathe in and notice how your body feels. Allow any tension to be released through your out breath. When you are ready, again, find your self in an outdoor setting and look for the mansion. Go up the stairs once again, open the doors and go into the foyer. This time you will see that in the hallway there will be more than three doors. There may be many doors. Find the one that calls to you. You will get a clear knowing of which door it is to open. Know that this is the one that will have an inner guide waiting for you. In your mind's eye, open the door. No matter what is there, ask if it is your inner guide. If the answer is "no," then ask it to take you to your guide. If this being answers yes, proceed by asking the question you may have for him or her. Trust whatever it is that comes forward. I remember one man had a cartoon character for his inner guide, and it gave him valuable information.

* * *

Planes and Highways

I often ponder the conundrum of time and its many dimensions. My linear mind wants linear answers. For example, in the story above, how did Philippe come to have a scar on his face in his disembodied state, and how did Jennie happen to re-create it? Did he imprint it so Jennie could recognize him/herself? Could Philippe have been or be a Philemon traveling to his own future? Hank Wesselman, anthropologist, author and modern day medicine man, who, in his *Spiritwalker* trilogy, finds himself in a future self, Nainoa, 500 years from now. Conversely, Hank finds that Nainoa can "visit" Hank's consciousness and he (Hank) is able to show him his decedent's past, which is the life Hank is now living. From this future life and perspective of Nainoa, not all has gone so well for America 500 years forward in time. Robert Monroe, in his last book of his trilogy, *Ultimate Journey*, also finds that his Higher Self, which he called the "I-there," is really a more evolved self from his "future."

Chapter Four showed that quantum theory posits that every part contains a part of the whole, so the entire universe can be found in the grain of sand:

> To see a world in a grain of sand,
> And heaven in a wild flower,
> Hold infinity in the palm of your hand,
> And eternity in an hour.
> -William Blake (1757–1827)

Little did Blake know that science would someday support such esoteric wisdom. Metaphorically, since all parts are part of the whole, then all time is in the now. Past, present, and future exist in one form but in another it is all happening now. I graphically came to this understanding once when I was traveling. Looking down from the airplane I could see a vehicle on the road below. It occurred to me that I could see where he had been. I also could see where he was going. I could see that ahead of him, around a bend in the road was blocked and therefore he wasn't going to be able to continue on his journey. It occurred to me that from this vantage point that I was seeing this person's past, present and future—all at once! This is how time can all be happening now.

To extend the metaphor, imagine that there are layers or levels of roads, not unlike the overpasses and underpasses in major cities. Now imagine that there are vehicles traveling on all those highways, and that they are traveling at different speed limits on each of the highways. Let's say that each one of the layers of highways represents a vibrational level of consciousness, and each vehicle symbolizes a lifetime. From the vantage point of the plane, in a higher dimensional plane (excuse the mixed metaphor!) one would be seeing all the lifetimes all at once. I believe the psyche is like this. It has the capacity to "zoom in" wherever it wants to for its own sake. Extending the metaphor even further, let's imagine that those vehicles not only represent your own life, but the lives of others as well. This is why we can have precognitive dreams and why psychics can pick up on the "road" that has the most energy with respect to one's choices. Going back to the one car on the one lane road with a bend and a roadblock, let's imagine that life is like this, full of roadblocks. Perhaps if the road had a fork in it, looking ahead I might be able to "feel" which road had the most energetic pull and be able to guess which one the vehicle would take, all the while understanding that in the universal web of life many other aspects come into play and therefore changes the "future."

I am sure that this is an oversimplified metaphor of how time works and how the psyche finds the perfect life to re-live; however, this conceptualization has helped me in understanding one possibility of the nature of time and of the collective or universal mind in the web of life. One thing is clear to me though, when a person enters one of these highways from a subjective reliving of a life, the objective psyche comes back with a new understanding and wider view of the world and ourselves. And, more importantly, we are changed by it.

Shamanic Travels

Another way to inner guidance is through shamanic journeys. Shamanism is possibly the world's oldest religion, and shamen are certainly the world's most experienced intuitives. Traditionally, the shaman has had the role of the psychopomp in their community. These ancient priests were sought out by the villagers when someone was ill, or in need of soul work. Shamen led initiatory rites and ceremony for their people as well. They were well acquainted with the Invisibles and the ancestors, relying on them for guidance and help in their journeying.

These persons of indigenous traditions seem to have mastered physics in liminal zones. A shaman is defined as "a person who is able to perceive the realms of souls, spirits, and gods, and who, in a state of ecstatic trance, is able to travel among them, gaining special knowledge of that supernatural realm."[15]

Mircea Eliade, one of the world's authorities on shamanism, was the first to coin shamen as "technicians of ecstasy." Eliade was not using the word ecstasy in the modern sense of "rapturous joy." He used the word "ecstasy" in its literal, etymological sense: "ec-stasis, out of the station, out of place, away from body," states Dianne Skafte. Skafte, author of *Listening to the Oracle*, indexed every example of Eliade's use of the word and found that his examples clearly do not refer to the joyous, as rapture can be filled with "terror and dread."

One of the distinguishing features of the shaman is his ability to travel interdimensionally and project his consciousness into other realms. That he or she can travel consciously among spirits and return with sacred information for the benefit of his society is what is important. Another feature of shamanism is that typically there are three levels of travel into the realms of spirit. As stated earlier, these three levels of the universe consist of the upper level, the lower level and the middle level. Each one of these realms has specific differences and has known roads of travel that access the three worlds. Often, the shaman is accompanied by helper guides who assist him from one realm to another. Shamen use spirits or familiars to help them successfully perform their tasks. These guides are seen as crucial to the retrieving of information or the healing work performed by the shaman.

Shamanism represents the most ancient systems of mind-body healing known to humanity. Archaeological evidence suggests that shamanism has been around at least twenty or thirty thousand years.[16] A shaman functions fundamentally the same no matter where in the world—"as guardian of the psychic and ecological equilibrium of his group and its members, as intermediary between the seen and unseen worlds, as master of spirits, as supernatural curer, etc. The shaman is able to transcend human condition and pass freely back and forth through the different cosmological planes."[17]

The ancestors also play a large role as source of help or guidance for the shaman. Eliade states:

> It follows that the souls of the dead, whatever the part they have played in precipitating the vocation or initiation of future shamen, do not create the vocation

by their mere presence (possession or not), but serve the candidate as a means of entering into contact with divine or semidivine beings (through ecstatic journeys to the sky and the underworld, etc.) or enable the future shaman to share in the mode of being of the dead (p. 85). In the world of the shaman seeing a spirit, either in a dream, vision, or awake, is a sign that one had transcended the profane condition of humanity.[18]

Is it Real or Memorex?

Shamen do not distinguish the real from the unreal. "In shamanism, one is conscious in the altered state and able to act purposefully within it. Shamen invariably report their encounter not as hallucinations or fanciful imagination but as experientially valid: what happens during the spirit-journey is *real* in that dimension."[19] Sometimes, however, shamanic rites are filled with danger and power plays. Malidoma Somé, in his autobiography, *Of Water & the Spirit*, tells of one occasion when shamen were gathering from other tribes. He is describing how shamen from other tribes might use their power to inhibit the power of another. He talks of an invisible dart, called a *lobir,* that can be thrown at another the plural of which is *lobie.*

"The *lobir* can take any form. The most primitive is an object that is thrown into a person's body. The most advanced is a living thing ranging from a lobir the size of a worm to one as big as the practitioner can guide."[20] What follows is a narrative of what happened on the day of Somé's grandfather's funeral:

During the second day of Grandfather's funeral the *nimwie-dem,* "those who have eyes"—medicine society members, initiated people, and some people who had an exceptional eye for observation—kept tabs on what was happening around them so that they could take appropriate actions. An ordinary person cannot see *lobie.* To have that ability you either have to know how to use them or be immunized against them. To the average person, *lobie* might look like something as harmless as the sun's rays, but to trained seers they might, for example, appear as a multitude of tiny shooting stars, traversing space at varying speeds. Some of the "stars" disappear when they hit a human body.[21]

Then a group of beings approached the funeral that was described as "short creatures," which seemed to look more like gnomes than humans from his description of them. When the whole tribe saw them they were frightened and screamed "The Kontombili!" When they saw these beings the women hid behind their husbands while the men looked down as if frightened.

Somé continued:

Ignoring the crowd, these bizarre beings moved toward Grandfather's *paala* and gathered around it in a semicircle with an air of solemn homage. My grandfather had told me many stories about these beings, but this was the first time I had actually seen any of them. Though they looked tiny and helpless, the Kontombili are the strongest, most intelligent beings God ever created. Grandfather told me they are part of what he called "the universal consciousness," but even though they are immeasurably intelligent, like us they too do not know where God is. They come from a world called Kontonteg, a fine place, far bigger than our Earth, yet very difficult to locate in time and space. They make their homes in illusionary caves that serve as the portals between our world and theirs. When the boburo and healers in our tribe need their counsel, they perform rituals in caves to access the world of the Kontombili.[22]

How are we to comprehend this kind of story? Do the *lobie* exist as thought forms? And if they exist as subtle body-thought forms, does the shaman have training that can energize them to the point of them being dangerous? Does this mean that they have a travel route through a field of some sort? We can see that the shaman's interdimensional travel corresponds to a nonlocal, non-space-time dependent archetypal field. The archetypal field has a form, structure, or pattern that can be accessed through specific ritually induced motions that access these patterns and therefore become the highways upon which shamen travel.

As Somé points out, we Westerners are bereft and out of touch with the natural world, and his people are horrified that we do not honor our ancestors, nor do we look to them for guidance. It is a perspective worth some contemplation. If we are to take seriously the *mundus imaginalis* as a realm, a careful examination of it might expand our way of seeing, experiencing and being.

Hermes in the Underworld: Where Angels Fear to Tread

As we saw in Somé's account with the Kontombili, it is not uncommon for the shaman to be shown by the gods how society came into existence, how the worlds were formed, and how man has a privileged and special relationship with the gods. In Castenada's controversial book, *The Teachings of Don Juan*, he quotes Don Juan:

> We believe to be "out there" is only one of a number
> of worlds. It is in reality a description of the
> relationship between objects that we have learnt to
> recognize as significant from birth, and which has been
> reinforced by language and the communication of
> mutually acceptable concepts. This world is not the
> same as the world of the sorcerer, for whereas ours
> tends to be based on the confidence of perception, the
> brujo's involves many intangibles.[23]

The Western world seems to be quick to jump on the bandwagon when it comes to quick fixes, and power journeys into ego-trips via shamanic power, accumulated perhaps by a few trips to an indigenous culture and a few trips on a hallucinogenic. This may be the Western shadow of shamanism. I have yet to see anything written that emphasizes or speaks to the shadow side of shamanism itself. It seems that in various cultures there are regular wars with neighboring shamen, who fashion spells, throw *lobies* left and right, and have their brand of shadow in the form of ego, power, and unconsciousness. Perhaps the widespread interest in altered states and indigenous cultures is a reflection of the yearning Westerners have for deeper inner religious experience and meaning.

However, it is possible to get entwined in the "magic" of shamanism, where power can reign over the ego, ultimately disregarding the underlying journey of the soul, or perhaps it may be another facet of the soul's lessons. Nevertheless, as a paradigm regarding the universal field, the world of the shaman does indeed seem to have a deep understanding of how to manipulate matter and travel in realms or dimensions that appear as ontologically real as the Western consensual universe. While Jung proclaimed these manifestations of spirits and demons originated from the collective unconscious, in the world of the shaman they are as real as any other reality and can be moved in and out of just as one would travel the highways and byways on our city maps. There are realms that exist in the Otherworlds that have a very dense vibration. Lost souls often reside here and one can feel sucked down in this plane. The film *What Dreams May Come* depicts this realm very graphically and has been described by many in their shamanic travels. It is the realm where having helpers would be important if you are caught there, and it's why the shaman always calls in ancestors and familiars before journeying.

Like the shaman, I know that we can ask for help from our ancestors, and guidance from the beings that live in the realms outside our every day awareness. Whether entering an altered space through drumming, chanting or in silence, it doesn't really matter when we have been touched by the other, those that we begin to notice when our subtle body responds, when our intuition states, "Pay attention, someone—or something—is here to give you important information!" I have learned to still my mind when I feel the familiar chills of another being in my presence, and I listen to know whether it is a passing spirit, or one that may be wanting to make contact for my evolution. Only once did I feel that I had been in the presence of the demonic, and I quickly invoked the light of protection.

This section is provided as information for new journeyers into the thresholds for knowing what to do when encountering the unexpected is important. This is why if you follow these traditions, they are usually accompanied by a teacher who can be of help when you enter a realm where help may be needed. I recommend that if you want to explore these realms more deeply, but feel a bit shy because of this warning, find a teacher who will guide and teach you what you need to know as a fellow traveler. There are many shamanic workshops and trainings that are available now more than ever before. While I could give you an exercise, I feel it would benefit you more to go to a workshop by a trained shamanic traveler, and then perhaps you can continue journey on your own.

Chapter Six

Awakening the Intuitive Self

All material substances are composed not only of observable matter, but also of more subtle field components with organized energy patterns, boundaries, and definitions. The deeper one probes into physical substance, the more one encounters the underlying electrical energy or the energy field.
-Dr. Valerie Hunt *Infinite Mind*

The Subtle Body Antennae

Why is it that in certain situations or in particular locations, such as at sacred sites, we experience goose bumps or an electrified feeling? What is the nature of these bodily antennae? I believe it is the human energy field surrounding and interpenetrating the human body that allows us to receive "information." We have seen that every living thing has a vibrational signature and a corresponding vibratory rate. This spectrum or frequency is also found in intersecting bands around the human body. This subtle body energy field—sometimes referred to as the *Light Body*—is the key to threshold occasions and subsequent transformation. It is the "device" we use to access portals of energy and their realms of frequency. Therefore, developing this part of yourself is paramount to eliciting the kinds of experiences I have been sharing with you throughout this book.

Our subtle body antennae work like a radio, which picks up signals from the airwaves, or we might say, different band-lengths in the universal field. We experience these frequencies through the channels of our body, the chakras being the stations. Some have likened the physical body as the strongest station, while the other stations represent the astral, mental, causal, and spiritual realities.[1]

These stations or bodies are the harmonics of the human energy field and must be fine tuned to "hear" and "see" clearly. Itzhak Bentov, author of *Stalking the Wild Pendulum*, contends that we must develop this mechanism to be able to interact with the different levels of consciousness corresponding to the different levels of the field. He further states that the Higher Self is the "spirit within us," and being part of the Creator, the higher levels are all connected and communicating with each other…The Higher Self cannot effectively interact with a physical body that has not been properly developed. It communicates with the psyche or the soul. It takes many lifetimes with a sustained effort to develop ones consciousness to a point at which direct interaction between the personality and the Higher Self becomes possible. At that point, the person becomes guided directly by the Higher Self, relying more and more on intuitive knowledge, which is funneled to him directly from the highest possible source.[2]

Further, Bentov believes that becoming spiritual has to do with refining the nervous system, which by doing so will reach a level of consciousness to a point in frequency that will resonate with the highest levels of creation. He states that this automatically entails the development of inner moral values and of the heart.[3]

Linking spirituality with the human nervous system parallels many of the Eastern traditions embracing meditative practices and yoga. In these practices the strengthening of the nervous system through the breath is practiced to hold the Kundalini when it rises, which is an opening of consciousness and connection to the divine within us. Prana yana yoga is one such practice that works with the breath in meditation to strengthen the energy bodies in order to be purified for the opening of Kundalini. Kundalini is said to be a powerful process that can cause involuntary movements, physical changes that are either painful or blissful, and leads to a total transformation of the personality. It is a spiritual awakening and therefore can be considered a threshold experience.

Energy medicine is becoming a vital aspect in healing fields today. Likewise, subtle body energy is finally being acknowledged as a fundamental element in healing paradigms in Western healing modalities. Eastern traditions have long known the relationship of *prana, chi, mana,* or the universal life energy present in and around the human body, recognizing it as the source of our health and vitality.

The subtle body is a nonphysical psychic body that is "superimposed" on our physical bodies.[4] It is said to flow along invisible meridian lines called *nadis* in the human body. When the flow is obstructed or weakened, disease and lack of vitality is the result.[5] (This is a common statement in the realm of the healing arts. Richard Gerber, M.D. and author of *Vibrational Medicine*, supports this claim throughout his handbook of subtle-energy therapies. I strongly recommend this book to anyone involved in the healing arts.) The word *subtle* has been used technically to indicate what is not material. Goswami, a Kundalini yoga adept and author writes:

> This is a subtle aspect of energy that has been called *prana.* "Pranic energy is directed through the system of numerous channels, called *nadi,* -the subtle nervous organization of the psychic body." The *nadis,* or the system of *nadis,* have been described at the subtle nervous systems of the psychic body.[6]

Therapeutic touch modalities in bodywork are also aware of the energy blocks contained in the field and work toward releasing these so the body—all of the energy bodies—are strengthened. The idea is that if the physical template is cleared energetically, you become free of the pollutants of the mind and body and of patterns that keep us locked in unhealthy states. This allows for consciousness and awareness toward the soul's evolution. I have found that holographic journeying, holotropic breathwork, and subtle body energy work—of which there are many— are a few of the ways of releasing energy blocks and patterns in the subtle body. Shamanic soul retrieval work is another energetic framework that also can release unwanted energy patterns and return "lost" parts of ourselves back to us that were lost to us in traumatic situations over our lifetimes.

Since the physical body is formed around and within the energy body, it is not surprising that distortions to the pattern can affect the way in which the physical body functions, producing symptoms we recognize as illness, says author and shamanic practitioner, Hank Wesselman. This reveals that the causes of virtually all illnesses are ultimately to be found within the life experiences of the sufferer. This conveys that the primary problem is not the illness, but rather the distortions caused by the loss of personal power or soul part that allowed the illness to invade the body and manifest itself in the first place.[7]

Interpenetrating Fields

Understanding how fields live within fields can be mind-boggling. Authors Mathew Fox and Rupert Sheldrake describe in their book *The Physics of Angels* how the universal fields interpenetrate with one another in a simple manner. They write, "The room in which we are sitting is filled with the Earth's gravitational field, which is why we're not floating in the air. Interpenetrating the gravitational field is the electromagnetic field, through which we see each other, which is also full of radio waves, TV transmissions, cosmic rays, ultraviolet rays, all sorts of invisible radiations. They also don't interfere with one another. Radio waves interfere with one another only if they're at the same frequency. But all the radio programs and TV programs in the world coexist, interpenetrating the same space."[8]

The key word is "frequency." Every living thing has a "vibratory signature" that constitutes "windows and thoroughfares."[9] Dr. Valerie Hunt is an intuitive with the gift of clairvoyance. She is also a physiologist whose research at UCLA documents physiological reactions through field transactions. Hunt states that all material substances have fields because they are composed of particles, atoms, and cells, and they are in constant dynamic equilibrium. This is why healing in the levels of the field can potentially create molecular changes. Hunt rejects the belief that vibrations of the universe interface with our body vibrations solely through the brain, as some scientists speculate: first, because the brain has a limited spectrum of cycles per second—zero to 24; and second, because she actually sees how the body interfaces with energy through the subtle body field, specifically through the chakras.[10]

Barbara Brennan, an atmospheric physicist formerly with NASA and current leader in energy body healing as well as author, cites two studies in her book, *Hands of Light*. This research by Dr. John White and Dr. Stanley Krippner lists many properties of the Universal Energy Field (UEF): The UEF permeates all space, animate and inanimate objects, and connects all objects to each other; it flows from one object to another; and its density varies inversely with the distance from its source. It also follows the laws of harmonic inductance and sympathetic resonance—the phenomenon that occurs when you strike a tuning fork and another one near it will begin to vibrate at the same frequency, giving off the same sound.[11] Here we have the key to synchronistic events and experiences.

As you can see, the notion of sound, vibration, and frequency become important and integral considerations when speaking of the human energy field or the subtle body.

The subtle body is not a new concept. Mystics and yogis have referred it to for thousands of years, having its origins in Hinduism. There are several synonyms for this human energy field; it is often referred to as the aura, auric field, and the astral dimension in Hindu cosmology. It has also been connected to *chi*, or *prana*, seen as the vital life force in and around all things. In the ancient Chinese doctrines *Chi* is described, as "a vast sea of energy in which we are all immersed and which penetrates every cell of our bodies."[12] Nearly all indigenous and spiritual traditions have a word that describes this life force.

The notion that natural healing forces are found in all living organisms is not a new idea in Western culture either. In ancient Greece, Hippocrates speculated that invisible emanations might be an aspect of a natural healing force found in all organisms and perhaps in the very air we breathe.[13] Paracelsus, a pioneer in the use of anesthesia, "held that an invisible fluidlike substance termed the *archaeus* permeates all parts of the body and provided it the nutriment for strength and health…Furthermore, all things are immersed in what he termed the *liquor vitae*, a vital force—this force…'was not enclosed in man, but radiated within and around him like a luminous sphere and it may have been made to act at a distance.'"[14]

Another pioneer was Anton Mesmer, from the 18 th century, who is usually known for his work with what he called "animal magnetism," and is also considered the father of hypnosis. Mesmer believed that everything in the universe is immersed in a universal fluid. A physician and student of Freud, Wilhelm Reich, came to similar conclusions in his concept of orgone energy. Reich thought of orgone energy as a universal substance that "mediated other forms of energy and could be controlled for purposes of improving both physical and emotional well-being."[15]

Jung referred to the subtle body as the "somatic unconscious." He said that the subtle body exists beyond time and space but consists of matter that is unable to be perceived.[16] Jung thought that the subtle body was the manner in which the notion of transference in psychology was transmitted from one person to another.

Chakras: Portals in the Human Body

It is nearly impossible to speak about the subtle body without referring to the chakras. The chakras are *specific* energy patterns, or centers, within the human subtle body, are often described as vortices (wheels) in Eastern cosmologies, and are sometimes depicted as lotuses in Eastern literature. These energy vortices can be seen by the inner eye by those who have developed their inner vision and actually resemble the lotus flower. Author and adept, Goswami, says that the chakras have been known to the mystics and yogis for centuries, even though Western medicine has refused to acknowledge these energy centers. These spiraling fields of energy, he states, form snake-like movements, which direct pranic energy in and out of the corresponding organs influenced by each center.[17]

These corresponding organs refer to specific glandular systems in the human body. Each vortex is situated in the spinal cord or nervous system and extends out of the physical body as energy portals that intersect with the seven levels of the subtle body field. Seen with the inner eye these portals rotate at different speeds depending on the health of the individual. Intuitives can often see these energy centers rotating and work with them to charge them and clear them for vitality and health. Someone who is ill may have energy centers that are either shut down or are rotating backward. When medical intuitives report seeing dark clouds of energy in the auric fields they believe that this indicates poor emotional or physical health.

These centers are gateways between various dimensions—centers where activity of one dimension connects and plays upon those of another dimension. This action, in turn, plays upon our activities in the outside world and *governs our interactions with others.* "As we experience the opening of a chakra, we also experience a deeper understanding of the state of consciousness associated with that level," states Anodea Judith, author of *Wheels of Life.*[18] This is the general theory for most all body/energy-healing systems.

Exercise #8

Finding Your Grounding Cord

Connecting with the Earth's energy is a primary tool to working with energy. You are not using your own energy once you have connected with Earth's energy. Also, it is always available and by consciously asking to connect with it you will do so, as we have seen that thought follows energy. There are several ways you can connect to the core of the Earth with your own energy cord.

First, begin by breathing deeply and as you exhale imagine that you have a cord of light energy that descends from the base of your spine and goes directly into the core of the Earth. You may be sitting or standing to perform this exercise. Some people like to imagine a cluster of crystals that reside at the core of the Earth and that your energetic cord can tap into this place. Imagine that the Earth's energy can now travel up the cord into your body and rejuvenate and revitalize you. As you practice this exercise daily, you can begin to notice an instant charge of energy that comes into your body.

Constance S. Rodriguez, PhD

I will give you another grounding exercise or tool in the next chapter that requires a little more concentration and practice but is well worth doing.

* * *

Anatomy of the Light Body

There is one more system I want to describe before integrating all of this with the universal energy field. This field is interconnected with the chakra system, yet is distinct from the chakras. Actually, these are differentiations of the subtle body field also referred to as the light body. I love what one of the leading persons working with therapeutic touch and author of *Spiritual Healing,* Dorothy Kunz, and says about the human energy field:

> The human field is much like a musical symphony. The musical dynamic is expressed in terms of inner consistency and harmonic relationships, no matter how dissonant the individual elements appear. Within the field, energies continuously circulate and flow outward and, sometimes, inward. The basic physical energy or vitality comes from what is called *prana* in Eastern philosophy. Prana enter the body through the vital counterpart of the spleen (not the actual organ, which in fact may be missing or damaged) and is modulated and distributed by a field mechanism known as a chakra (wheel), which may be called energy "transformer." The solar plexus chakra transforms this prana into the vital energy which is so important to the physical body.[19]

Kunz describes the different "notes" of the field saying that there are four basic fields in the subtle body system: the vital field, the emotional field, the mental field, and the intuitional field. Brennan, author in *Hands of Light*, actually breaks these fields down even

136

further, stating that there are seven levels, each corresponding with the seven chakras.

What follows is a verbatim description of these fields from Kunz's work, *Spiritual Healing*. Her description of the various qualities is worth repeating in detail:

> *The Vital Field*: The physical body is surrounded and permeated by the vital (etheric) field, which attenuates at about one to six inches from the body or two inches on the average. This field is an intrinsic part of the body itself.

> *The Emotional Field*: Interpenetrating both the physical field and its vital field is the emotional field. This field is wider in scope, extending about eighteen to forty-eight inches beyond the body. Thoughts or intentions can enlarge its normal ovoid shape to express the strong feelings projected by the person— elasticity is one of its major characteristics . . . As it projects out, and if another emotional field is there, it tends to interpenetrate the other's emotional field and thereby affects the other person's feelings.

> *The Mental Field*: The individual's mental field is part of a universal mental field and interpenetrates the emotional as well as other fields. The mental field can be described as representing one's intellectual functioning. It reveals one's ability to visualize and rationalize or conceptualize, to think clearly, and to synthesize or make meaning out of one's experiences.

> *The Intuitional Field*: The intuitional field is omnipresent and, like the other fields, permeates the whole universe. . . The action of this field can be likened to soft, beautiful music that we cannot hear through the din of our daily lives.

Each one of these fields may be compared to the spectrum of light in which there are different vibratory frequencies or wavelengths different in degrees and densities.[20]

Finally, Kunz suggests that there are variations of the whole human field, just as there are variations in the spectrum of white light. She states, "The fields continuously interact with one another through the chakras and they are also affected by the fields of others."[21]

Intuition, Altered States, and Subtle Body Awareness

Subtle body, or "Light Body" work as it has been called, has been most helpful to me in deepening my understanding of the application of the healing that takes place in energy fields. Recently, I entered a yearlong training to deepen my understanding experientially of the body and its levels of fields. Not only did I literally gain hands-on experience with energy fields, but also began to understand them from a lived sense. During my training program I was studying Brennan's *Hands of Light* volume and one paragraph in particular became an "aha" experience for me. It answered some of the questions I had been holding while working with all of this material. Brennan had found that each chakra and each level of the energy field exhibited different frequencies, and the key was to learn how to shift frequency bands to see into each level of the field.

This idea relates to Hunt's "vibratory signatures carried in the structure of its field." Hunt gives an example of how this might work. She states that thought is an organized field of energy composed of complex patterns of vibrations, which consolidate information. She continues, "If the accompanying emotional energy is strong, the field is energetic and integrated. It persists and stimulates other fields to action, both the dense world of matter and other human beings. If one uses auditory memory skills to decode an information field, one hears sounds or voices. If one translates thought through visual memory, one sees pictures. And if one processes vibratory information via olfactory or kinesthetic memory, one smells odors or has a motion sensation."[22]

Thoughts entrain other thoughts of similar vibrations. Theosophist, Elbert Benjamin, writing in 1926 states:

> "All mental processes are governed by the *Law of Association.* Among the most powerful associations by Resemblance is that of identical or similar resonance. This is the key to making contact with things or thoughts . . . on the inner plane; for their thoughts and things having the same vibration are together. Distance on the inner plane is of a different order than in the physical world; there it is measured by disparity in vibratory rates."[23]

Immersion in the spiritual experience has the ability to actually change the physiological laws of the body. There are indigenous cultures, including Native American cultures, whose rituals take the people into deep altered states. During these states, those in the ritual can have long needles pushed into their bodies, which produce no pain or bleeding. These practices are believed to bring one closer to their God source, and the piercing is a culmination of the ecstatic state. Scientists have tested yogis who are able to move into these deep altered states and have demonstrated this needle piercing. They have found that the yogis are in a deep theta wave pattern when hooked up to an EEG brain monitor (an electroencephalograph machine), which shows the brain waves of the yogi. Whirling dervishes of the Sufi orders are known to dance their way into these states of being. As a group ritual, many participate in the piercing at the height of the ecstasy.

Looking at the universal field in group situations, Bache, author and prior professor of religion and philosophy, speaks about "phase locking" among people and their chakras in group situations. This phrase borrowed from science means that when something is vibrating at the one frequency different from another, it begins to entrain its self with the other in an integrated resonance. We have all heard that clocks begin ticking at the same time after being in a room together for a length of time. Bache is saying that when people enter a sufficiently deep pattern of resonance with each other it produces at highly integrated group consciousness.[24]

I believe that tribal cultures live in this "phase-locked" condition because of the cohesiveness of their acute knowing of what is happening with each other and with the "other," which is outside of our Westernized waking consciousness. Remember the example of the Kontombili that Malidoma Somé described in Chapter Five? Perhaps as a group they lived in this phase-locked resonance, explaining why they would all see the same things with the inner eye.

Bache gives a beautiful example of the phase-locked condition of the unified field that constellated during his classes:

> The atmosphere in the room becomes supercharged, and everyone seems to congeal into a superunified state . . . . I sometimes have the acute sensation that there is only one mind present in the room. It is as if the walls that usually separate us have become gossamer curtains. Individual persons melt into a softly glowing field of energy, and this unified energy *thinks* and *feels* and *hungers to speak*.[25]

Others have described the field experience as a felt change in the quality of space between them, as though it becomes charged with electricity. This is my experience when a field is ignited and my body responds to alert me to its presence. This field is more than a psychic experience—it actually has a physiological template that is an expression of the subtle body. A felt sense or bodily response is a reliable indicator as to when the field has been activated.

It is interesting to me that in body/energy work that the hands are used as the instrument by which one feels into these fields leading to "information" about that particular field, such as in the Light Body work I referred to earlier. However, it is not only through the hands that information is accessed. Information is also accessed through various "preceptor sites," which are specific to the chakras as well as to the "level" of the body field that I discussed earlier. The vital, mental, emotional, and astral levels intercept each chakra. For example, a person may have sexuality issues that are usually correlated with the second chakra. In a clinical setting, the clinician may experience the issues through the emotional field, which may be experienced as eroticism in the field, or between the clinician and client. Because these specific sexual issues are experienced by the clinician through a felt sense, the clinician would be tuning in through the second level of the field, the emotional field. However, if these same issues were to be perceived visually, then the clinician would be tuning into the mental level of the field. Actually, these issues may be perceived and accessed at any one of the subtle body levels, and can be accessed simultaneously. This is why some people have an intuitive sense; others may have imagery, having developed their perceptive skills at one level or the other. I have noticed that when I am working I access information at various levels of the field, sometimes emotional levels, or the astral level, sometime visually and often viscerally. Occasionally I will hear certain phrases or words that "pop" in.

According to the Eastern cosmologies regarding chakra systems and embraced by nearly all of the physical body therapies and therapeutic touch modalities, each chakra is related to a group of particular psychological issues pertaining to that energy pattern. And as we have seen, energy patterns involve a kind of frequency at each level that the trained eye (inner eye) or hand, as the case may be, can actually read and interpret. These energy patterns emit energy at different Hz or light waves with corresponding colors. Reading or tuning into the differences in energy patterns at each level of the chakra, and then determining which level of the subtle body (vital, emotional, etheric, for example) one is tuned to, is an example of the intricacy of the training in subtle body energy that I participated in. Many body therapies bring in the psychological correspondents that have been developmentally determined in the physical body as well as the subtle body form. Much of Barbara Brennan's work, for example, is modeled after bioenergetics, a form of psychotherapy that incorporates character structure both physically and psychologically.

Although we can speak in metaphors regarding the universal field, or even bring scientific language to describe it, such as "molecular changes, energy transactions, information transfers, and frequency patterns," none of these words impart the remarkable quality of the transformative, numinous moments that occur in the interactive fields. These synchronistic moments are powerfully felt experiences that leave you in awe of its mystery, and I am grateful when these experiences occur in my work and life. There always is an "other" quality to the experience, which also holds a mystery of the unknown, and I hope always will. Perhaps this is also a condition of being when working in the subtle energy fields.

Unlike the radio analogy, these fields have a transformative, numinous quality that is unforgettable. People have reported dramatic openings. Self-awareness may come in slowly or instantaneously, wherein we are transformed down to our very bones.

It is evident that to participate in the numinosity of threshold space, we must open and clear our somatic antennae, our energetic channels, so we can be free to experience the multidimensional realities within our grasp—by simply changing the "station."

Exercise #9

Creating a Healing Template

Sit quietly with your intention set for information or help with a particular issue. Breathe in and connect to the Earth, finding your grounding cord. Ask for an image that you will be able to use to help yourself heal or for another person's healing. Always ask that this be in the highest good for your soul self or for the other. Sometimes suffering is aligned with soul lessons and ought not to be tampered with. You do not have to be concerned with this issue if you ask first that you be given help from the Source and that it be in the best interest of the soul.

Asking for an image may be as simple as seeing a broken arm mended. You will be placing this template onto the thing that is to be healed. I have a friend who told me she asked in her meditation what she could do to help with a fire that ravaged the Earth in her area one summer. She was given an image of green plants sprouting up from the charred Earth. She was told that by using this template, or image, every time she thought of the fire, she would be helping the Earth to heal faster. There are many situations you might think of to use this wonderful energetic healing tool for yourself, others or the Earth and its "hot" spots.

Chapter Seven

Waking the Inward Eye

Allegory of the Cave

Imagine a cave very far underground with a long passage leading out into the daylight. In this cave there are men who have been prisoners there since they were children. They are chained to the ground, and even their heads are fastened in such a way that they can look only in front of them, at the wall of the cave, behind the line of prisoners a fire is burning, and between the fire and the prisoners there is a roadway. People walk along this road and talk to one another and carry things with them. The prisoners would see the shadows of those people, shadows thrown by the light of the fire on the cave wall in front of them. And, supposing the cave wall reflected sound, the prisoners would hear sounds coming from the shadow. Since the prisoners cannot turn their heads, the only things they will see and know are shadows; and so they will assume that the shadows are real things, for they cannot know anything about the fire and the roadway and the people behind them.

Now suppose we unchain one of the prisoners, and make him turn around. This will be very frightening and painful for him; the movement of his body will hurt him, and his eyes will be dazzled by the fire. And if we tell him that the things he now sees are more real than the shadow, he will not believe us, and he will want to sit down again and face the wall of shadows which he understands. Now, suppose we go even further then this, and forcibly drag him out through the long tunnel into the sunlight. This will be even more painful and frightening for him; and when he arrives above the ground he will be blinded by the sun. But slowly, let us imagine, he will get used to it. At first, he will be able to look at the stars and the moon at night. Later he will look at shadows thrown by the sun and at reflections in pools of water. Finally, he will be able to see the trees and mountains in full daylight, and he will recognize that these, not the shadows in the cave, are the real things. And when he has become accustomed to looking around him, he will at last realize that the light which makes all this possible comes from the sun.

And now, of course, he will be sorry for his fellow prisoners in the cave, and he will consider himself much luckier than they. If he were to be suddenly brought back to the cave, his eyes would be unaccustomed to the darkness, and he would no longer be able to recognize the shadow. His fellow prisoners would say that his experiences had ruined him, and they would consider him a fool for going out into the daylight.

-Plato's Republic

The Nature of Reality

We are often like Plato's prisoners, chained to our beliefs and thoughts about the reality of the universe. Throughout this book I have been proposing different lenses with which to see realities. I owe a debt of gratitude to Hank Wesselman for the following material.

In his workshop on Hawaiian Mysticism, he shared very simple and easy explanations of the nature of reality given to him by his

Hawaiian teachers. The Hawaiian medicine people, or shamen, believe that there are four important levels to understanding reality. I have often come across these four levels in other traditions as well, and although there seem to be more, these are the levels we are to be concerned with now in our evolution of consciousness.

The first level is the physical level. It has to do with ordinary reality. Every thing has a beginning and ending, cause and effect, and a sense of separation in this level. It is the reality that we have been most concerned with in Newtonian science over the past 300 years. It concerns "Chronos" time, or linear time, and it is the level in which the universe is subject to a developmental thrust. This thrust includes human development moving through the process of evolution.

The second level is a subjective level. It is the level of thoughts, emotions and feelings. They can't be measured as of yet, but nevertheless we feel them, experience them, and they are real to us. This is the level of psychic awareness and energy. It is the level where all things are connected energetically through what the Hawaiians refer to as the "*aka*" field, or the universal energy field. Shamen can actually see this field of energy as an existing grid, web or net. It is made of filaments of light that are like strands of energy that connect with and to all things. What is important is that the more you put your energy or thought into something, the more the *aka* builds up. So that in essence, the energy field in sacred sites or places of worship, for example, has an accumulation of *aka*. This is the underpinning in the manifestation of will, that it's bringing form to what you desire. When you hear form follows energy or thought, this is what happens. An actual field builds until it is magnetized where form or matter is attracted to it. *Aka* in Hawaiian means "shadow" or "reflection." Shamen throughout history have known that this field of energy is a reflection of all things; it is the primordial stuff out of which everything in the universe is created. In science, it is referred to as "dark matter"—a mysterious energy that is thought to keep everything together. This is the template that Jung referred to as the Unitarian Web that underpins synchronistic events.

Recently I was able to see this primordial energy field. Lying on the beach, I was very relaxed and gazing at the white clouds painted on the blue sky. Suddenly, my vision shifted and I could see millions of light particles moving about. It was very beautiful and I was able to watch the "light show" for a long time. I thought that perhaps these were the filaments that sometimes cross over my physical eyeballs, but I could see those as well. My energy from this sight shifted and I felt as if I had connected with the smallest living particles the Hawaiian medicine and healers throughout time have spoken about.

Level II, unlike Level 1, has no beginning and no ending. It only has cycles and transitions and is based on the thermodynamic law that no energy is ever lost. This is the level wherein past lives live. It is in this level that all time is now, and all things are happening outside the linear time veil of "before and after." It is why we can tap into other lives, as well as our own and re-experience them as if they were happening now. This is the dimension where consciousness is nonlocal, and moves around via the *aka* web of frequencies throughout the multidimensions of reality.

Level II is also the level of manifestation. It is here that we can create thought forms and by giving it *chi* or *prana*—we can magnetize the thought form so that it becomes dense, which the universe will then respond by bringing the thought form to you. This is why it is so important to be clear of negative thoughts in your daily spiritual practice. This practice is very powerful and can work in the opposite direction as well, for what we focus on can become manifest. Energy follows thought, therefore it is important to put worry aside. The unconscious does not make decisions, it cannot say, "oh, he doesn't really mean that." The Hawaiians refer to this part of our being as our *Ku*, which acts as our instinctual being and has a beautiful built-in capacity to do what the conscious mind, or the *unconscious mind* asks. Sometimes this is why saying affirmations do not work, because there may be another part of the psyche, an unconscious part, that has a different agenda. As an example, fear or other thought patterns from the ego or in the unconscious mind can get in the way of producing a congruent and focused thought needed in manifesting.

The *Ku* is also the domain of the physical body. It interfaces with the inner and outer worlds; it never sleeps, and it never "lies." It is the part of us that perceives subtle energy, or is the antennae connected to the physical realm that brings in information even when we are not consciously aware of it. For these reasons psychologists say that 90 percent of our communication is through nonverbal cues. The *Ku*, according to Hawaiian mysticism, is what mediates between the

Oversoul and the *Lono*, or conscious mind. This interface is where intuition arises. The interesting thing about this aspect of our being is that it takes everything as real; therefore, our imaginal travails are very real to the *Ku* and this is why it has a physiological affect, just as our dreams can produce a physiological response when we feel frightened, waking up with our hearts beating and our pulse racing.

Level III is the level of the spirit world. It is the level of dreamtime symbols and archetypes. "It is the level where everything is a part of a loom or tapestry that is being woven together and meaning is determined by relationship," says Wesselman. It is the level where you determine your reality, where everything is what you think it means. Here when the ego assigns meaning, it is what it means to you. This is the level of astral travel as well as the level of shamanic travel.

Level IV is about cosmic experience. It is where the mystics speak of rapture, bliss and ecstasy. It is the level Rumi, as well as other mystics, wrote about in their prose and poetry. It is the level when you are no longer "you" but exist as a part of the Sacred Mind, of the All That Is. It is the level of the source, sometimes referred to as Christ consciousness, cosmic consciousness, or Buddha Mind. There are other names given to this experience as well.

Developing the Intuitive Self

The key to developing the intuitive self is through the channels of the body. Finding bodywork that is specific to clearing the energy bodies and chakras will accelerate the opening of the intuitive self. This sometimes means years of release work, breathwork, "past-life" work, as well as other modalities specific to depth psychology and meditation practices. Along with the development of an aware ego, the purpose of this work is the evolution of the soul, which allows the larger Self, or Oversoul, to be the captain of the person's journey while here. To be able to open the intuitive self for the evolution of our being and soul we need to have a clear energy body. Our subtle body is the interface between the inner and outer worlds. It is the gateway between psyche/soma and the *animus mundi*, or world soul.

An exercise given to me by a modern day medicine woman, whose teacher was Native American, taught me this breathing exercise to clear and charge the chakras. There are many exercises to clear chakras, but this is the one I practice the most. It is important as I said before to have a clear receiver to develop the intuitive mind. This exercise can be done while sitting and practiced before meditation. With eyes closed, and hands face down on your lap (to keep the energy in your body), use your breath and intention to clear your energy field. While taking a breath, visualize that you are using your breath to move up the back of your chakras, beginning with the root chakra at the base of your spine all the way to your crown chakra above your head. At the crown chakra hold your breath to the count of four, then release your breath slowly, this time visualize it coming down the front of your chakras until you reach your root chakra again. Repeat this breathing exercise several times. This will energize you and at the same time will clear your chakras.

Another important tool for the moving in and out of fields of awareness is grounding. Grounding can be done in several ways, but again I will share with you the technique I use the most. This involves the hara—located a couple of inches below the belly button—and engaging the pranic tube that runs through your body. (Barbara Brennan has devoted a large portion of her second book, *Light Emerging*, to the hara and how to engage it). First, begin by standing gently, knees bent slightly so that you are resting your pelvic area on an imaginary seat. With your intention, send your energy into the middle of the Earth and find a spot to anchor it. Once you have anchored your energy imaginally (using your intention) in the middle of the Earth, imagine that a tube of energy can now come up from the Earth and energy can flow up this tube into your body. You may have a very felt sense of a slower moving energy. Once you feel this spot it is like being plugged into a great wall socket. Bring it up to your belly, where the hara is seated. This is the place of power and can be charged with energy. Many tai chi and qigong practitioners use this place to harness Earth energy. Moving your pelvis around a bit sometimes helps to find the connection with the Earth and the hara. You will actually feel a vibration in your body if you "plug" in properly. When this energy begins moving up my body, I begin to feel warm immediately. Next bring this up through your body and connect it to the crown chakra. Now imaginally, open the crown center and shoot the energy up through a small upside-down funnel that exists about 2 ½ to 3 feet above your head. This now connects you to your higher source. This powerful energy source is the energy that healers often connect with before doing energetic healing.

Although these tools may seem simplistic to some of you, they are the prerequisites for activating and inviting the sacred into your life. I would be remiss in not mentioning them.

Activating the Gateways

There seem to be specific gateways by which you can move into the threshold of the interactive fields. There are at least three conditions that invite the universal energy field into our awareness. First, a shifting of consciousness must occur. The time/space continuum must shift from linear (Chronos) to acausal time (Kairos). This *abaissment*, a lowering of consciousness, means quieting the activity of the ego into a receptive state of awareness. You are simultaneously alert and still. You want your ears wide open and your eyes soft. It is a place of reverie and of waiting, and invitation. It is as if you open a door, inviting in whatever wants to cross over into the realm of ego from other layers of the psyche and collective unconscious. It is important to practice this with curiosity when opening thresholds states. It is like a diffusion of consciousness that requires a shifting of gears. It is a downshifting of sorts. I will give you some specific exercises to initiate opening these doors later in the chapter. It is also important to invoke the "white light," which accesses an energy vibration of protection.

Second, you must have a "stable attractor site." Bache states that this stable attractor site can be a person, place, or thing and its magnetic quality can be enough to induce an archetypal field. You will recall this experience of persons who attest to this at sacred sites around the world. In a personal conversation, author Christopher Bache, shared that he has had the experience in teaching wherein a template for the field constelled in each class he taught and was re-initiated more easily every succeeding semester in his classroom.

150

Through repetition—and perhaps reverence—over time, a template forms from which information can enter consciousness through the subtle body substrate. As noted earlier in this chapter in my discussion on the subtle body, this information can inform you through imagery or visually, kinesthetically, or through oracular means. This stable attractor site can be a sacred site in the outer world and/or the inner world. Through repetition, the site itself becomes magnetized. Perhaps it is a specific room in your home or an altar where you have a sacred place or spiritual objects that become the stable attractor site, inviting an alchemical vessel for transformation.

Third, it is important to set an intention for the field to form. Intention is powerful medicine. It contains energy and vibration, and creates an integrated resonance inviting sacred space and inner guidance. Once the field becomes ignited, it feels very alive. The atmosphere changes, and there is a felt sense of it. The numinosity of the field brings goose bumps to all who experience its occasion, and its mystery creates transformation for those in its presence. These are the main features or conditions that I have been able to identify when entering a threshold place.

Keys to the Psychonoetic Field

One of the ways in which I journey to receive inner guidance is through my imaginal sacred garden. It is important to develop a sacred place in the outer world and one in the inner world. This establishes a "stable attractor site" and serves as a way to prime the pump for interactive imagery and visits to the Otherworld realms. I use this with people in taking them into past lives, or as a "launching pad" for traveling to other realms. It is also used in shamanic work as a place to begin before entering the middle world, upper world or lower world.

My *stable attractor site* is an imaginal sacred garden that shifts and changes with my inner needs. This garden has a beautiful goldfish and koi pond with a waterfall as its central feature. It has a wonderful turtle that is sometimes sunning himself on one of the rocks around the pond. It also has colorful flowers, cymbidium orchids, and ferns that shimmer next to the pond. Surrounding the pond are a few Gold Coast pines that give a sheltered feeling in my garden. To the left of the pond is a large flat rock, one that I can lay on to sunbathe or to go to other places. I also have an imaginal standing stone that anchors the garden and is an altar where I place gifts I have received from my inner travels. At the base of this stone is a beautiful crystal and nautilus shell that I was recently given on one excursion to an island in the middle world realm. Just beyond this standing stone is an arbor covered with red roses. When I walk through this arbor I can often walk down to a sandy beach where I meet with my inner advisors. Sometimes I will bring a problem or concern to them and we will sit on the sand in a circle while I am advised of what I may need to think about or do.

I give you this descriptive picture of my sacred garden so that you can see just how specific and sensually detailed it is. It is a very real place for me and I often go there to be rejuvenated. I love watching the fish in my pond and they know me so they greet me when I come. Recently I went there and found a beautiful yellow and black snake coiled up on my horizontal slab enjoying the sunshine.

Often we can invite our familiars to our garden, or they sometimes just appear. I have an orange cat, in spirit now, that lives in my garden. He was a cat that came and laid down next to me during a breathwork session at someone's home in waking life. After that particular session, he followed me out to my car and jumped in. I was "adopted" by him that day and, naturally, brought him home with the permission of his previous owner. After that whenever I felt blue or was journeying in my room with my altar, he wanted to be in there with me. "Furball" only recently passed through the eternal threshold and I was delighted to find him residing in my sacred garden.

Learning to Listen

When I first began to explore the world of the inner realms, I wanted to "hear" what my guides and inner beings wanted to say to me. To learn to hear, I first began to practice listening by doing what is called automatic writing. This practice began with using my nondominant hand, and invoking the white light for protection from unevolved denser forms of energy, which may be standing by. At first it was slow going. I felt energy come through my arm and circle once or twice around on the paper. I practiced holding the pen very lightly and letting go of the muscles in my arm. I patiently would wait and soon the circling would begin. As I began to formulate questions out loud or internally, the pen would move and a seemingly different voice with a very unusual dialect would come in and write the answer to my question. Soon, as I practiced this, I could "hear" the answers internally before my hand would have time to write them out fully. After awhile and as I began trusting the inner voice, I started feeling that the writing was becoming too laborious. One day, I was also told to stop relying on the automatic writing and instead listen through my meditation. This became the way in which I could trust the inner voice as one outside of my ego. I was often delighted and inspired by the answers that seemed to come from higher sources and were ones I came to rely on. Over time these guides seem to change and others come in to give guidance.

Remote Viewing

People often tell me that they feel as if they are making it all up, especially in Holographic Journeying. What I say is, that is okay, go ahead and make it up. It is still coming from your psyche, and your psyche chooses these "made up stories" for a reason. After a while the imagery will become spontaneous. This is why guided imagery is helpful in the beginning as it "primes the pump" so to speak. One of the ways you can tell if you are receiving intuitive hits or information is when the information or image just "pops" in. After asking a question, I will receive an image or message. It comes in, rather than my consciousness creating it.

I often used remote viewing to develop my inner sight. I began with "looking" at my house on my way home from my office during the winter months when it was dark early in the evening. I would imaginally look to see if the lights were on, and which ones were lit. For example, I would look to see if someone had flipped on the outside lights, or if just an inside light was on. Often, when I arrived home I had a positive "hit." Then I also began practicing this with my mailbox. My post office was out of the way and I didn't want to make a wasted trip if nothing was in my postal box. I started using the "green light, red light" imagery. This is just like a green light or red light at stop light intersections. If I asked if I had mail I needed to pick up, I would either see a red light or green light. To further test my remote viewing I began to ask to see if there was mail sitting in the slot and if I needed to pick it up. I began to get positive "hits" with this method as well. The more that I practiced the less often I was wrong. From these experiences, I had immediate feedback on my ability to "see." I needed these experiences for myself in order to trust what I was seeing later on.

Holographic Mindfulness

This exercise is important to develop the focused concentration needed to explore things in detail while out on journeys. You might say it is a way to examine something with a close-up lens. This is a practice that many traditions say develops the sharpness of the mind as a tool to meditation and manifesting.

First, bring something into your space that you want to practice holding in the mind. It could be a flower, or a photo. Anything really. Look closely at it, and then close your eyes and see it in your mind's eye. Open your eyes again and see if you got it correctly. Again, close your eyes, and this time begin to examine all sides of it. See the back of the top, and the bottom. Now open your eyes and physically examine it. See how close you come to seeing it correctly. When you feel you are able to do this easily, next try the room you are in. Look at the room carefully, where all the items are in place, the feeling of the room, the temperature of the room. Next close your eyes and re-create it. You will have the room to verify your senses. After a while you can go on to other ways of seeing holographically. You may want to visit your office or your friend's house. Never do this without permission. Bring your friend into focus imaginally and ask them if you can journey to their house. You will get a definite "yea" or "nay."

Sometimes the image will turn its back giving you a "no." If you get a yes, you could actually call after your remote viewing visit and get verification of the experience. This is another way to practice clear seeing and experience your inner eye.

It is important that when embarking on these exercises that you partner with your inner critic. This analytical and sometimes cynical self can often get in the way of your trusting what you are seeing or hearing. Our inner critics develop early in life in order to protect us. This part of ourselves can have a very loud voice if we are not in charge of it and aware of its presence. You can hear its voice when it says things like, "you are just making this up," or "you don't really think you can do this, do you?" This part of ourselves can really put a damper on a wonderful experience. I suggest that you acknowledge this inner voice, and hear what it has to say about your desire to develop your intuitive self. Then politely acknowledge that you have heard its concerns and then ask it to wait until you have completed the exercise to make its comments known. At that time you can revisit this voice and see what it may have to say about it all. But remember, the inner critic is trying to protect you and often has opinions driven by fear. You have the option of listening but not agreeing with its opinions! I have sometimes mentally put the inner critic in a chair outside my door to wait until I am complete with my journey or travels.

Active Imagination

Active imagination is another skill that is important to develop to invite inner guidance and awaken the inner eye. Active imagination is when the imagery interacts with you. I call this interactive imagery. In interactive imagery, the symbols, images and beings talk to you, give you information visually, or you may internally "hear" information. This often happens spontaneously through shamanic drumming, or when entering a sacred inner garden, or sitting at an altar.

Some people find it helpful to enter the imaginal realms through shamanic journeying. In shamanic journeying, people are invited or instructed to ask for a power animal as a guide or helper in future journeys. This power animal becomes your ally is subsequent journeys for healing or gaining information on a requested subject. In these kinds of experiences, your power animal may communicate with you telepathically and vice versa. This interactive imagery feels "real" and meaningful. It is happening to you rather that you making it happen.

Using your intention and attention, the images begin to actively engage you. While some people like drumming as an entry point, others enter these threshold states through meditation. I most often go into meditation through the breath. Deepening my awareness and moving into non-ordinary consciousness through the breath has become second nature to me. I always ask for guidance to come in through the "highest vibration" or through Christ consciousness. When I feel the familiar sensation of the energy of the "other," I then ask or make my request, either for healing of myself or others, or for information. When I journey, I often use the sacred garden imagery as a starting point, and journey to another time, to spiritual realms or to the upper world, or sometimes my power animal will meet with me and take me to a realm. Sometimes, as I said before, I walk down a path and meet with my spiritual advisors, usually in a circle on a "beach." The portal, or way in which you journey, doesn't really matter as much as what it is that you bring back with you from these inner landscapes of the soul.

I started my career working with children. Using art as a method of healing and discovery, I would sometimes ask children how they felt about something. Because words are not the medium of choice with children, I asked them to draw a picture of their feelings. Sometimes I would draw a thermometer and have them show me where on the thermometer they felt they were as a gauge between feelings. For example, I once asked a child to show me on the thermometer how the anger in her family felt to her. I said, "if '0' is no anger and at the top indicates a lot of anger, where is it in your house?" Children were very good at having a visual image to tell about what things felt like. Sometimes I would just ask them to visualize a thermometer and they would give me an answer, instead of actually drawing it. From these experiences, I would also begin using the thermometer to give me answers to questions I might have. This seems to work well with questions that need a gauge of sorts, or something that shows somewhere in between a "yes, and "no," which muscle testing can't do. Muscle testing here refers a method of asking the body a question and testing for strength or weakness of the muscles for a "yes" or "no" answer. (See more below regarding Donna Eden's book, *Energy Medicine*, or purchase a copy of *Map: Medical Assistance Program*, by Machaelle Small Wright, for more information on how to do this for yourself.)

Body Talk

Another way we can receive information is through the wisdom of our body. Hawaiian medicine people say that the *Ku* resides in the body. Our bodies have an innate knowing that, if we will bother to ask, can give all sorts of advice. I have gone to chiropractors that practice a type of kinesiology that involves asking the body what it is lacking or what it is allergic to. To this end, the practitioner places one of various vials of substances on the body and muscle-tests it for strength or weakness. If the arm tests strong, the answer is "yes" to the given question and a weak muscle indicates a "no." Donna Eden, author of *Energy Medicine,* gives examples in her book on how to muscle-test for many things. When I first learned this technique I used it on everything and for everything. I also began asking questions to my inner guidance about esoteric things, or questions concerning lost items. This technique has proven to be very helpful. I have used it to request dates for setting up workshops and conferences, or to ask where in my garden a specific plant would like to live.

Another one of my favorite books by Machaelle Small Wright is *Behaving as If the God in All Life Mattered*. In her book, Wright also talks about a "yes" or "no" muscle-testing technique in which you put your thumb together with your small finger creating a circuit. After asking a question, using your other hand, you insert your forefinger and thumb together into the circuit created by the first hand. While asking the question, a "yes" question will create a strong circuit, causing the muscles of the fingers to hold together firmly. A "no" answer will create a weak circuit and the muscle will give way to opening the circuit.

Constance S. Rodriguez, PhD

I am a passionate gardener and in the spring, you can always find me out in the garden. In wanting to work with the nature spirits and devas of the vegetable and flower kingdom, I often asked questions about what a new plant or flower would like in terms of living in its new home.

One spring morning, after I had planted my vegetable garden, I was besieged with earwigs. They seemed to be eating everything that popped through the soil. I was getting frustrated and didn't know what to do, and the yes/no technique was not bringing me answers that would stop the problem. As Wright learned from her Findhorn gardening experience, we can contact the deva of the plant kingdom and ask for help. This particular morning, I sat down near the green beans as they had been severely eaten by the time they reached a couple inches high. After shifting into an altered state, I asked to contact the nature spirit in charge of the green bean family. Immediately, I felt a surge of energy come into my being. It was a very tight and highly refined energy. It felt like millions of insects buzzing furiously and instead of hearing them, I could feel them. It was truly a foreign energy and not very comfortable to me. I felt that I had made contact with the *Green Bean* deva! I told this elemental what the problem was and asked if it would find a way to give the earwigs only a few of the seedlings instead of all of them. I told the Green Bean goddess that I would like to have a harvest in the summer and would be grateful for its help. I thanked it for coming and then planted a few more seeds.

Soon they showed their tiny green sprouts and I watched to see if they would be eaten. They grew and grew. Only a few of the seedlings were nibbled on. That summer I had a beautiful green bean harvest and thanked the deva each day for its help. Even though it sounds a bit humorous, this experience touched me deeply. Before this I felt as if I was able to get information just through muscle testing and had no *lived* experience of the elemental kingdom. After this experience, I became aware that my intention and request was regarded with care by the elementals and that I truly am only one tender of the garden. This kingdom affects the physical realm. We need only ask.

Dreamwork How-To's

The dreamscape provides another entry point into Otherworld realms. I recently met a man who told me that he has been lucid dreaming since he was a child. In these dreams he is very aware that he has been given all kinds of information and experiences from Otherworld guides. He often would write down all that he was being taught, and even kept a tape recorder handy because the information was flowing so quickly that he couldn't keep up with it all. Finally, he asked that they slow down, and allow him to sleep, as it was interfering with his need for a restful sleep. Lucid dreaming is a method of dreaming in which we are aware of being in the dream world and can move around freely just by the thought. It is a consciousness interactive dream.

One of the ways to receive guidance, unfettered by the ego, is by consulting the dream psyche for its help. People who are having a difficult time with something and need an answer often request a dream to give them further guidance. I talked earlier about the guidance several people had received through their dreams. I would like to give you specific keys now toward understanding and remembering your dreams.

We can enhance dream recall in several ways. First it is important to set the intention to remember your dreams. If you want to incubate a dream for a specific question, it is important to write about the problem at hand and then before falling off to sleep, ask your dream psyche a specific question related to the problem. This is usually enough to bring a dream that will point to the direction needed. If you are unsure of the answer, find a dream buddy to process with. Getting your association to the symbols or images and asking how these are like something in your waking life feelings is a key to opening the dream and finding meaning with the imagery. There are many excellent dream books on the market and classes and I encourage you to begin to unlock your own dream imagery.

Setting the intention is very important to activate the dream. Another important technique to let your dream psyche know you are serious about remembering the dream, is to place a pen and paper next to your bed at night. In the morning, before making any movement whatsoever, ask yourself, have I been dreaming? This is often enough to bring the dream back to you. Dreams are like mice; they scamper away at a moments notice, but usually if we can grab the tail (tale) end we can bring them back into full awareness. Sometimes you may be left with only a dream snippet, yet this is almost always enough to gain some insight, as it is somehow full of concentrated associations. I also tell people to drink lots of water before going to sleep, and this will wake them in the middle of the night to use the bathroom. I often remember dreams during this middle of the night interruption.

I have found that once the dream psyche knows that I am serious by writing down every little dream I can remember, more and more dreams seem to come forward each morning. Recall just becomes part of the morning and I feel gifted by the enormous depth occasioned by each dream. They are filled with levels of meaning that sometimes require many visits back to my dream journal to unravel the dream's entire message.

Dreams are another portal into Otherworld realms as well. I believe we visit shamanic worlds during dreamtime. I remember once being carried off by a fairy, who seemed to be taking me to his world. I was so startled by the reality of this experience that I woke up, heart beating wildly and stunned that it was happening in dreamtime. I believe I was visiting the lower world. In shamanism the lower world is the world of the elementals, of the ancestors and of the familiars who are called upon by the shaman whenever they are journeying for the purpose of helping their people. Another time, I was met by my deceased mother who was very much alive in this plane of reality. She told me she was fine and loving her new life. She looked very vibrant and happy. When I came back I felt as if I had been with her and felt renewed by her visit. Over the years of working with people's dreams, many people have told me of these "dreamtime" experiences and have felt the reality of the loved one's presence.

Other kinds of dreamscapes involve the "upperworld" where guides, teachers and souls live. These realms are accessed in journey time as well, but when they are occasioned through the portal of a dream they feel very numinous and important. No matter when people have had these kinds of dreams, they recall them instantly. It is as though we are gifted by the numinous presence of a loving being who knows us fully. The love and presence of these beings is transformative by itself alone. I believe we are in the presence of our Oversoul when we have had one of these kinds of experiences. When a dreamer tells of this experience in my classes or groups, there is a silence that follows, and the room feels energized as if by the telling of the dream the divine enters the room. These kinds of dreams cannot be interpreted. It does not work to try to ask for associations or amplifications of the image. These are Otherworld dreams.

When we are visited by the Other in dreamtime, it feels very different than the kinds of dreams we usually have that show us the way or give guidance through our amplification of the imagery. It is as if we are being dreamed. To be visited by the world psyche is to be impressed upon by its aliveness, and reality. Like the visit of a familiar, or a totem animal, it has its own reality, and sometimes there may not be a "message" for the dreamer. Sometimes when the world psyche wants to be heard it will enter our dreams asking simply to be noticed, or to hear its lament, as happened when my clients were having dreams of being in foreign lands oppressed as women right after the 9/11 terrorist attack in New York and Washington, DC.

These are a few of the ways you can begin to tune in and pay attention to your intuitive self. All of them invite the inward eye to awaken and soon you will find synchronicity a wondrous daily event. It feels like living within the divine flow of all that is and there is a sense of the magical. Life becomes full of helpers and beings involved in the dance of evolution. When we all participate at this level we all participate in the healing of ourselves, each other, and ultimately the sentient Earth being, the planet herself.

Am I Making it Up?

I am asked this question all of the time. "How do I know if I am making it up or not?" First, know that it is your inner cynic that asks this question. You might want to ask this part of you to allow you to enjoy the imagery as if it were a movie before this part of you can come in with its comments. This proves helpful often with people who want to have an experience but do not know what it will be like and or feel that it has to be a certain way.

Second, remember that the imagination is a *key* that allows entry into the imaginal realms. When I go into my sacred garden in my mind, I am imagining it. Once I am there, however, the imagery begins to take on an active life of its own. The images speak to me, move about, and so forth. So give yourself permission to make it up!! After all, it is your movie! Whatever you make up counts, as the *Ku* knows no difference. In other words, your instinctual self does not differentiate between what is "real and not real" To your instinctual body, it is all real. In Western culture, we do not trust things that are from imaginal places. We have been acculturated to think that the imagination is not to be trusted. See if you can let that belief go when moving into the imaginal realms, where things and beings begin to interact with you.

I often find that once I have moved through a threshold into the imaginal realm, the images I am having want to show up in certain ways. As an example of this, let me tell you of one experience I had that concerned this book. I had sent a proposal to a publishing agency and was told I may have to wait four to six months before hearing back from them. Every so often, I would "remotely" go to where my manuscript was, and I would *see* it under piles of other manuscripts. Every once in a while, I would check in and see where it was on the pile. One day, in this interactive imagery, I saw that it was opened on someone's desk. I thought, "Well, maybe I just want it to be opened," and tried to imaginally "close" it. It wouldn't close. I could imagine it closed but then it would pop back open. This experience usually confirms for me that what I am seeing lives more in "objective" reality than not.

A Few of My Favorite Things

Wesselman says that our *Ku* loves beauty. When we connect with beauty, we automatically can connect with our Oversoul. The *Ku* and the Oversoul are closely connected and one elicits the other. The *Ku* also loves sensate things. Our instinctual body will tell us when it wants rest, sex, play, or an ice cream cone. It is childlike in its nature yet contains our creativity and joy.

I decided to make a list of my favorite things that my *Ku* loves. They are my passions in life, which include gardening, lying in the sun at the beach, visiting my sacred garden, the smell of the roses when they are in bloom; stargazing in a hot tub, exploring new lands, places, and exploring sacred sites. The anticipation of the journey ahead is a favorite feeling. I love meeting the inner others as they bring guidance and synchronicity to my daily life. These are a few of my favorite things. When you have time I suggest you make a list of yours, for they act as energizers to the sacred within you. Like the icons on a computer desktop, once you tap into these images you open them up, you are already entering a threshold within which to dance. May your journeys unfold to bring you richness, may your passions bring you joy and may your intuitive Self become second nature.

Blessings on your journey.

Constance S. Rodriguez, PhD

To contact the author
or for information regarding her programs
See her website:
www.soulmatters.com

You may order this book directly
from 1st Books Library at:
www.1stbooks.com

Glossary

Abaissement du niveau mental This refers to a <u>lowering</u> of consciousness, It is a shifting from the mental level to an open, unthinking way of being, not unlike being in reverie or in a meditative state. It is like shifting from "left-brain" thinking to "right brain" thinking.

Active Imagination A Jungian term that refers to a process whereby the individual enters an imaginal state where imagery arises. The images then begin to have a life of their own and can interact with the individual. Information is given and shared. Jung believed that we also confront the shadow parts of our psyche in active imagination and believed this and dreams were essential ways to get to know the unconscious parts of our psyche. He differentiated active imagination from guided imageries or fantasy where images that emerge can change form. In active imagination, although the image has autonomy, it stays true to form.

Animus Mundi The world soul or soul of the world.

Chakra A Sanskrit word for wheel. It usually refers to the disc-like energy centers that emerge and revolve from out of the body. The adepts see them as extending out of the body in the front and back. They are not acknowledged as orthodox energy centers in Western medicine, yet have been known for hundreds of years in the East. There are traditionally seven chakras although some systems describe more. These vortices are connected to the glandular and meridian systems in the body. There are many volumes written about the chakra and corresponding levels of the human aura or subtle body field.

Chronos   Also spelled Cronos, was known as the God of time. In Greek mythology, Cronos was the youngest son of Uranus and Gaia. He was said to have ruled over Earth and Heaven. He is also identified as Saturn, the old man that sits on the throne in the heavens.

Collective Unconscious Also referred to as the "objective psyche." Carl G. Jung is known for the origination of the term the "collective unconscious." He wrote volumes on the collective consciousness and it is foundational to his work. I will not be able to give justice to the vastness of this concept but will give a very brief overview. The collective unconscious refers to all that which is outside the personal conscious and *personal* unconscious. It contains archetypal images and the instincts, which pertains to all humankind, as well as the cosmos. Jung said that there exists a second psychic system of a universal, impersonal nature that is inherited and gives definite form to certain psychic contents and can come through to the personal conscious or psyche. He termed this the collective unconscious

Complexes   These refer to core traumas rooted in the unconscious. It is like an emotional cluster of energy that creates a field effect. People who are gripped by a complex usually will have a strong emotional reaction to something or someone. In the everyday jargon, you may hear of someone having a "father complex." This has to do with someone who has unresolved pain, for example, regarding his/her father and may project these feelings onto people he/she does not know.

Deva   A god or good spirit. A spirit guide. Celestial power. Mountains, trees, and plant kingdoms are said to have corresponding devic kingdoms overseeing the well being of these places and sentient beings. It may be that the devas are what intuitives "tune into" when receiving information about places and things.

Eternal Now This term refers to all time existing in the present moment. It is opposite of linear time, Chronos time. It is a way of thinking of time as holistic, where the present, past and future is all happening in the "now." See "Planes and Highways" in chapter 5 for a working metaphor of this idea.

Noetic (s) Noetic is a Greek work meaning to know through the intellect, wisdom, mind spirit and soul. Christian de Quincey, professor of philosophy and consciousness studies states that noetic sciences refers to the exploration of the nature of consciousness, particularly of the non-rational, intuitive aspects of consciousness and how it relates to the larger cosmos.

Nonlocality This term is used to refer an event in space-time that is unable to be measured. If something happens here that affects something there, but there is no mechanistic way of measuring this event, it is referred to as having non-locality.

Numinosum (Numinosity) Jung borrowed this work from Rudolf Otto's work in *The Idea of the Holy* (1958). It refers to an affective state or religious experience that is ineffable—without words. It brings overwhelming intensity to the experiencer and has the capacity to transform him/her. When people have had a numinous experience its impact is never forgotten.

Constance S. Rodriguez, PhD

Ontological (Ontology) The branch of metaphysics that deals with the nature of being or reality; the very foundation of reality.

Psychoid The deepest substrate of the psyche. A description of the autonomous functional systems of the unconscious as it becomes increasingly collective until they are universalized and where there is no differentiation between self, other and the world.

Sacred Mind Another way of talking about the collective unconscious. It refers to the transpersonal realms, or universal mind. It observes that there is a collective psyche that has a numinous quality. Christopher Bache, who coined the term, says to experience Sacred Mind even briefly profoundly shifts one's sense of identity because it gives one an entirely new reference point from which to experience life.

Subtle Body Sometimes referred to as the aura, causal body, or light body. Research is finding that there exists an unseen yet energetic field having substance around living plants and people. It has been discussed in the phantom limb experiments and photographed around plants that have been torn or damaged. Many researchers are describing this energy field as having a higher frequency with multidimensional octaves that can be tuned into consciously and "treated" or worked with, as in hands on healing modalities. Barbara Brennan, author of *Hands of Light*, is well known for her description of the subtle body having 7 interconnected levels, each connected with a chakra system and having a different function which generates physical, emotional and spiritual health.

Vesica Piscis An ancient symbol where two circles overlap, and create an inner shape called the mandorla. This symbol is said to represent the meeting of two worlds, heaven and earth, the inner and outer, the profound and the mundane. The mandorla can be thought of as the place between worlds, and is an image of the many portals in the liminal states.

Unus Mundus One world or cosmos

Constance S. Rodriguez, PhD

Index

Constance S. Rodriguez, PhD

Oversoul, xiii, 103, 114, 148, 161, 162
Panpsychism, 57
Perennial Philosophy, 73
Philemon, 49, 50, 103, 112, 113, 114, 120
Portals, i, xvii, 57, 114, 134
Prana, 130, 136
Psychoid, 168
Psychonoetic, xii, 151
Shamanism, 122, 123
Sheldrake, Rupert, 63, 132
Skafte, Dianne, iii, 30, 48, 123
Somé, Malidoma, 24, 27, 124, 140

Soul stories, 91
Subtle body, 138
Talbot, Michael, 68
the Intuitive Self, 129, 148
The Knights Templar, 117, 119
Universal Energy Field, 32, 133
Vesica Piscis, 168
Wesselman, Hank, xiii, 24, 120, 132, 145
Wilber, Ken, 71
Woodhouse, Mark, 55

About the Author

Dr. Rodriguez has taught and lectured both nationally and internationally. She teaches healing practitioners and psychotherapists the art of perceptual energy as a medium for healing the Body/Mind. With a background in Jungian Theory and Depth Psychology and as student of many traditions, her passion is in awakening the soul through Pathways to the Self. She has a wide interest in all forms of healing, specifically in the area of subtle energy. From personal, professional and theoretical experience she is well equipped to navigate you through the multidimensional energy fields outlined in this book. She maintains a private practice in Northern California.

Notes

Prologue

---

[1] Bentov, I. (1977*). Stalking the Wild Pendulum.* New York: E. P. Dutton. p. 91.

[2] Wesselman, H. (2001) *Visionseeker.* Carlsbad: Hay House. p. 42.

Chapter One

[1] Freeman, M. (2000)."The Flaming Door." *Parabola*, vol.25, p. 45.

[2] Ibid., p. 45

[3] Eliade, M. (2000). "Beyond the Precincts of the Profane," *Parabola*, vol. 25, p. 70.

[4] James, W. (1999, Paperback Edition). *The Varieties of Religious Experience.* New York: The Modern
Library. p. 256.

[5] Corbett, L. (1996). *The Religious Function of the Psyche.* New York: Routledge.
p. 23

[6] Bolen, J. (1979). *The Tao of Psychology, Synchronicity, and the Self.* New York:
Harper
& Row. p. 6.

[7] Jung, C. G. (1960). *Synchronicity, an Acausal Connecting Principle.* New York:
Bollingen Press. p .25.

[8] Von Franz, M.L. (1980a). *On Divination and Synchronicity, the Psychology of
Meaningful Chance.* Canada: University of Toronto Press. p. 98.

[9] Ibid.

[10] Woodhouse, M. (1996). *Paradigm Wars: Worldviews for a New Age*. Berkeley: Frog
Ltd. p. 183.

[11] Ibid., p. 183.

Chapter Two

[1] Jung, C. G. (1969). "On the Nature of the Psyche." In R.F.C. Hull (Trans.) *The Collected Works of C.G. Jung* (Vol. 8). 2nd edition. Princeton, NJ: Princeton University
Press. (Original work published in 1947), p. 217.

[2] Corbin, H. (1969). *Alone with the Alone*. Bollingen: Princeton University Press. p. 4.

[3] Kellogg, R. (1969). *Analyzing Children's Art*. Palo Alto: Mayfield Publishing Co. p. 78.

[4] Corbett, L. (1996). *Religious Function of the Psyche*. New York: Routledge. p. 146.

[5] Conforti, M. (1999). *Field, Form and Fate: Patterns in Mind, Nature and Psyche*. Woodstock: Spring
Publications. pp. 41–44.

[6] Delaney, G. (1998). *All About Dreams*. San Francisco: Harper Collins. p. 12

[7] Ibid., p. 12.

[8] Skafte. D. (1997). *Listening to the Oracle*. San Francisco: Harper Publishing. p. 116.

[9] Delaney, G. (1998). *All About Dreams*. San Francisco: Harper Collins. pp. 61-62.

[10] Bache, C. (2000). *Dark Night, Early Dawn: Steps to a Deep Ecology of the Mind*. New York: SUNY
Press. p 9.

[11] Ibid., p.74.

[12] Skafte, D. (1997). *Listening to the Oracle*. San Francisco: Harper Publishing. p. 116.

[13] Ibid., p. 30.

[14] Abram, D. (1997). *The Spell of the Sensuous*. New York: Vintage Books. p. 27.

[15] Ibid., p. 15.

[16] Avens, R. (1982). *Imaginal Body: Par-Jungian Reflections on Soul, Imagination and Death*. New York:
University Press of America. pp. 73–74.

Chapter Three

[1] Wilber, K. (1996). *Eye to Eye: The Quest for the New Paradigm*. Boston: Shambala. p. 45.

[2] Lemkow. A.F. (1990). *The Wholeness Principle: Dynamics of Unity within Science, Religion and Society*.
Wheaton; Il. Quest Books. p. 80.

[3] Woodhouse, M. (1996). *Paradigm Wars: Worldviews for a New Age*. Berkeley: Frog Ltd. p. 52.

[4] Ibid., p. 10.

[5] de Quincey, C. (2000). "Consciousness, Truth or Wisdom?" *IONS, Noetic Sciences Review, 51* (8), p. 11.

[6] Wilber, K. (1996). *Eye to Eye: The Quest for the New Paradigm*. Boston: Shambala. p. 155.

[7] Woodhouse, M. (1996). *Paradigm Wars: Worldviews for a New Age*. Berkeley: Frog Ltd. p. 183.

[8] Ibid., p. 155.

[9] Mansfield, V. (1995). *Synchronicity, Science, and Soul-Making*. Chicago: Open Court Publishing. p. 170.

[10] Ibid., p. 137.

[11] Lemkow, A.F. (1990). *The Wholeness Principle: Dynamics of Unity within Science, Religion, and Society*. Wheaton, Il: Quest Books. pp. 67–68.

[12] Ibid., pp. 68–69.

[13] Capra, F. (1975). *The Tao of Physics*. Boulder: Shambala. p. 59.

[14] Ibid., pp. 59–61.

[15] Ibid., pp. 62–65.

[16] Ibid., p. 66.

[17] Ibid., p. 67.

[18] Ibid., p. 67.

[19] Ibid., p. 68.

[20] Laszlo, E. (1993). *The Creative Cosmo: A Unified Science of Matter, Life and Mind*. Edinburgh: Floris
Books. pp. 35–36.

[21] Ibid., p. 39, 49.

[22] Ibid., pp. 47–78.

[23] Ibid., p. 48.

[24] Zinkin, L. (1987). "The Hologram as a Model for Analytical Psychology."
*Journal of Analytical
Psychology, 32*. p. 10.

[25] Ibid., p. 6.

[26] Laszlo, E. (1993). *The Creative Cosmos: A Unified Science of Matter, Life and Mind*. Edinburgh: Floris
Books. p. 52.

[27] Ibid., p. 57.

[28] Lemkow, A.F. (1990). *The Wholeness Principle: Dynamics of Unity within Science, Religion, and
Society*. Wheaton, Il: Quest Books. p. 115.

[29] Laszlo, E. (1993). *The Creative Cosmos: A Unified Science of Matter, Life and Mind*. Edinburgh: Floris

Books. p. 141.

[30] Ibid., p. 62.

[31] Sheldrake, R. (1988). *The Presence of the Past*. Rochester: Park Street Press. p. 198.

[32] Ibid., p. 199.

[33] Ibid., p. 199.

[34] Laszlo, E. (1993). *The Creative Cosmos: A Unified Science of Matter, Life and Mind.* Edinburgh: Floris
Books. pp. 63–64.

[35] Ibid., p. 64.

[36] Mansfield, V. (1995). *Synchronicity, Science, and Soul-Making*. Chicago: Open Court Publishing. p. 82.

[37] Laszlo, E. (1993). *The Creative Cosmos: A Unified Science of Matter, Life and Mind.* Edinburgh: Floris
Books. p. 148.

[38] Ibid., p. 148.

[39] Ibid., pp.186–187.

[40] Ibid., p. 191.

[41] Zinkin, L. (1987). "The Hologram as a Model for Analytical Psychology."
*Journal of Analytical
Psychology, 32.* p. 1.

[42] Progoff, I. (1973). *Jung, Synchronicity, and Human Destiny*. New York: Julian Press. p. 108.

[43] Jung, C.G. (1969). *The Archetypes and the Collective Unconscious*, Vol.9.1,
Princeton: Princeton
University Press. p. 173.

[44] Talbot, M. (1991). *The Holographic Universe*. New York: Harper Collins Publisher. pp. 2–3.

[45] Ibid., p. 3.

[46] Ibid., p. 31.

[47] Ibid., p. 31.

[48] Progoff, I. (1973). *Jung, Synchronicity, and Human Destiny*. New York: Julian Press. p. 46.

[49] Talbot, M. (1991). *The Holographic Universe*. New York: Harper Collins Publisher. p. 47.

[50] Wilber, K. (1985). *The Holographic Paradigm and Other Paradoxes*. Boston: Shambala. p. 44.

[51] Lemkow, A.F. (1990). *The Wholeness Principle: Dynamics of Unity within Science, Religion, and Society*. Wheaton, Il: Quest Books. p. 90.

[52] Talbot, M. (1991). *The Holographic Universe*. New York: Harper Collins Publisher. p. 47.

[53] Zinkin, L. (1987). "The Hologram as a Model for Analytical Psychology." *Journal of Analytical Psychology, 32.* p. 5.

[54] Woodhouse, M. (1996). *Paradigm Wars: Worldviews for a New Age*. Berkeley: Frog Ltd. p. 193.

[55] bid., p. 204.

[56] Wilber, K. (1996). *Eye to Eye: The Quest for the New Paradigm*. Boston: Shambala. p. 160.

[57] Ibid., p. 257.

[58] Woodhouse, M. (1996). *Paradigm Wars: Worldviews for a New Age*. Berkeley: Frog Ltd. p. 207.

[59] Wilber, K. (1996). *Eye to Eye: The Quest for the New Paradigm*. Boston: Shambala. p. 162.

[60] Wilber, K. (1985). *The Holographic Paradigm and Other Paradoxes*. Boston: Shambala. p. 253.

[61] Koestler, A. (1967). *The Ghost in the Machine*. New York: Macmillan Co. p. 205.

[62] Woodhouse, M. (1996). *Paradigm Wars: Worldviews for a New Age*. Berkeley: Frog Ltd. p. 186-187.

[63] Ibid., p. 185.

[64] Conforti, M. (1999). *Field, Form and Fate: Patterns in Mind, Nature and Psyche*. Woodstock: Spring Publications. p. 35.

[65] Ibid., p. 37.

[66] Gerber, R. (2001). *Vibrational Medicine: The Handbook of Subtle-Body Medicines*. Rochester: Bear & Company. p. 158.

[67] Conforti, M. (1999). *Field, Form and Fate: Patterns in Mind, Nature and Psyche*. Woodstock: Spring Publications. p. 47.

[68] Schwartz. G. & Russek, L. (1999). *The Living Energy Universe*. Charlottesville: Hampton Roads Publishing Co. p. 54.

[69] Woodhouse, M. (1996). *Paradigm Wars: Worldviews for a New Age*. Berkeley: Frog Ltd. pp. 187–188.

[70] de Quincey, C. (2002), *Radical Nature*. Vermont: Invisible Cities Press. p. 67.

Chapter Four

[1] Bache, C. (2000). *Dark Night, Early Dawn: Steps to a Deep Ecology of the Mind*. New York: SUNY Press. p. 133.

[2] Ibid., p. 159.

Chapter Five

[1] Hannah, B. (1976). *Jung: His Life and Work*. New York: G.P. Putman's Sons. p. 122.

[2] Ibid., p. 121.

[3] Jung, C.G. (1960). *Memories, Dreams and Reflections*. (rev. ed.). (A. Jaffe, Ed.). New York: Pantheon

Books. pp. 317–318.

[4] Hannah, B. (1976). *Jung: His Life and Work.* New York: G.P. Putman's Sons. p. 154.

[5] Ibid., p. 155.

[6] Romanyshyn, R. D. (2000). "Alchemy and the subtle Body of Metaphor, Soul, and Cosmos." In R.
Brooke (Ed.), *Pathways to the Jungian World, Phenomenology and Analytical Psychology.* New York:
Routledge. p. 27.

[7] Gardner, L. (1996). *Bloodline of the Holy Grail.* Rockport: Element Books, Inc. p. 256.

[8] Ibid., p. 256.

[9] Ibid., p. 257.

[10] Ibid., p. 257.

[11] Ibid., p. 257.

[12] Ibid. p. 266.

[13] Ibid., p. 264.

[14] Ibid., pp. 264–265.

[15] Drury, N. (1989). *The Elements of Shamanism.* Longmead: Elements Books, LTD. p. 6.

[16] Harner, M. (1980). *The Way of the Shaman.* San Francisco: Harper & Row Publishers. p. 40.

[17] Ibid., p. 41.

[18] Drury, N. (1989). *The Elements of Shamanism.* Longmead: Elements Books, LTD. p. 85.

[19] Ibid., p. 39.

[20] Somé, M. (1994). *Of Water and Spirit.* New York: Penguin Books. p. 62.

[21] Ibid., p. 63.

[22] Ibid., p. 69.

[23] Drury, N. (1989). *The Elements of Shamanism*. Longmead: Elements Books, LTD. p. 82.

Chapter Six

[1] Bentov, I. (1977). *Stalking the Wild Pendulum*. New York: E. P. Dutton. p. 84.

[2] Ibid., p. 93.

[3] Ibid., p. 94.

[4] Judith, A. (1994). *Wheels of Life*. St. Paul: Llewellyn Publications. p. 13.

[5] Ibid., p. 191.

[6] Goswami, S. (1999). *Layayoga: The Definitive Guide to the Chakras and Kundalini*. City, VT: Inner Traditions Publishing. p. 20.

[7] Wesselman, H. *Visionseeker*, Carlsbad: Hay House. p. 270.

[8] Fox, M. & Sheldrake, R. (1996). *The Physics of Angels*. San Francisco: Harper Collins. p. 42.

[9] Hunt, V. (1996). *Infinite Mind: Science of the Human Vibrations of Consciousness*. Malibu: Malibu Publishing Co. pp. 65–66.

[10] Ibid., p. 61.

[11] Brennan, B. (1987). *Hands of Light: A Guide to Healing through the Human Energy Field*. New York: Bantam Books. p. 40.

[12] Woodhouse, M. (1996). *Paradigm Wars: Worldviews for a New Age*. Berkeley: Frog Ltd. p. 191.

[13] Ibid., p. 190.

[14] Ibid., p. 191.

[15] Ibid., pp.191–192.

[16] Schwartz-Salant, N. (1982). *Narcissism and Character Transformation*. Toronto: Inner City Books. pp.
119–120).

[17] Goswami, S. (1999). *Layayoga: The Definitive Guide to the Chakras and Kundalini*. City, VT: Inner
Traditions Publishing. p. 20.

[18] Judith, A. (1994). *Wheels of Life*. St. Paul: Llewellyn Publications. pp. 13, 22.

[19] Kunz, D. (1995). *Spiritual Healing*. Wheaton, Il: Theosophical Publishing House. p. 216.

[20] Ibid., pp. 217–222.

[21] Ibid., p. 223.

[22] Hunt, V. (1996). *Infinite Mind: Science of the Human Vibrations of Consciousness*. Malibu: Malibu
Publishing Co. p.137.

[23] Hill, A.D. (1996). *Souls' Body: An Imaginal Re-viewing of Morphic Fields and Morphic Resonance*.
Unpublished doctoral dissertation, Pacifica Graduate Institute, Carpinteria, CA.

[24] Bache, C. (2000). *Dark Night, Early Dawn: Steps to a Deep Ecology of the Mind*. New York: SUNY
Press. p. 178.

[25] Ibid., p. 196.

Printed in the United States
16962LVS00004B/97-99